The Other in Perception

A Phenomenological Account of Our Experience of Other Persons

Susan Bredlau

Cover image: Paul Klee, *Episode B at Kairouan* (1931). Ink on paper mounted on cardboard. The Berggruen Klee Collection, 1984. © 2018 Artists Rights Society (ARS), New York.

Published by State University of New York Press, Albany

© 2018 State University of New York

All rights reserved

No part of this book may be used or reproduced in any manner whatsoever without written permission. No part of this book may be stored in a retrieval system or transmitted in any form or by any means including electronic, electrostatic, magnetic tape, mechanical, photocopying, recording, or otherwise without the prior permission in writing of the publisher.

For information, contact State University of New York Press, Albany, NY
www.sunypress.edu

Library of Congress Cataloging-in-Publication Data

Names: Bredlau, Susan, author.
Title: The other in perception : a phenomenological account of our experience of other persons / Susan Bredlau.
Description: Albany : State University of New York Press, [2018] | Includes bibliographical references and index.
Identifiers: LCCN 2017058929 | ISBN 9781438471716 (hardcover : alk. paper) | ISBN 9781438471723 (pbk. : alk. paper) | ISBN 9781438471730 (ebook)
Subjects: LCSH: Merleau-Ponty, Maurice, 1908–1961. Phénoménologie de la perception. | Phenomenology. | Perception (Philosophy) | Other (Philosophy)
Classification: LCC B829.5 .B686 2018 | DDC 121/.34—dc23
LC record available at https://lccn.loc.gov/2017058929

10 9 8 7 6 5 4 3 2 1

To my father, Carl Bredlau.
He took delight in learning and taught me to do the same.

Contents

Acknowledgments — ix

A Note on Citations — xi

Introduction — 1

1 Phenomenology — 5
   Introduction — 5
   Husserl and Intentionality — 5
   Merleau-Ponty and Embodiment — 11
   Russon and Polytemporality — 17
   Conclusion — 25

2 The Phenomenological Approach to the Experience of Others — 27
   Introduction — 27
   Husserl and the "Pairing" Relation — 30
   Merleau-Ponty on the Perception of Others — 34
   Russon and the Others within Our Own Bodies — 38
   Conclusion — 43

3 The Institution of Interpersonal Life — 45
   Introduction — 45
   Perceiving through Others: Neonate Imitation, Joint Attention, and Mutual Gaze — 45
   Infant-Caregiver Play Periods as "Pairings" — 52
   Caregiver "Availability" and the Impact of Pairing Relations on Infant Perception — 58
   Pairing and Trust — 62
   Russon on Pairing as the Institution of Personality — 64
   Conclusion — 69

4 Recognition and Sexuality	71
Introduction	71
Childhood Intimacy and Adult Intimacy	73
Sexuality as a Bodily Intentionality	74
Hegel on Recognizing Subjects as Subjects	77
Sexuality as Embodied Recognition	81
Sexuality and Interpersonal Vulnerability	86
Sexuality and Freedom	90
Conclusion	92
Conclusion: The Concrete Ethics of Lived Experience	93
Notes	97
Bibliography	115
Index	123

Acknowledgments

I am deeply grateful to the many people through whom I have become more attentive to and articulate about the rich significance of our experience. These relationships have had a profound impact on my writing of this book and on my life as a whole. I especially want to thank John Russon, whose encouragement and wise counsel have been, and continue to be, a vital presence in my world. I also want to thank Ed Casey, Kirsten Jacobson, Peter Manchester, Kym Maclaren, Donn Welton, Cynthia Willett, John Lysaker, John Stuhr, Laura McMahon, Whitney Howell, the anonymous reviewers for SUNY Press, Greg Kirk, Scott Marratto, David Morris, Don Beith, Michael Cox, David Ciavatta, Peter Costello, Joe Arel, Patricia Fagan, John Garner, Steve Arcas, Eve Rabinoff, Eric Sanday, Rachel Calef, Greg Recco, Christopher Rolling, Karen Robertson, Carly Yasinski, Jenny Chio, Ömer Aygün, John Tielli, Rhett Henry, Maria Talero, Alexa Cucopulos, Nathan Anderson, Chris Gale, Miles Rosenthal, Kerry Thompson, Jason Matteson, Bruce Gilbert, Janet Bredlau, Liz Bredlau, Jason Strawsburg, Amiere Strawsburg-Bredlau, and Ryan Strawsburg-Bredlau.

An earlier version of portions of chapter 3 was published as "On Perception and Trust: Merleau-Ponty and the Emotional Significance of Our Relations with Others" in *Continental Philosophy Review* (2016). https://doi.org/10.1007/s11007-016-9367-3. I am also grateful to Imprint Academic for permission to reproduce in chapters 2 and 3 revised versions of some portions of "Husserl's Pairing Relation and the Role of Others in Infant Perception," *Journal of Consciousness Studies* 23 nos. 3–4 (2016).

A Note on Citations

For Merleau-Ponty's *Phenomenology of Perception*, which is the focal text of this study, all citations will refer to *Phénomenologie de la Perception*, published by Gallimard in 2005 and to the translation by Donald A. Landes, published by Routledge in 2012. The page number of the French text is listed first, followed by the English page number.

Introduction

We do not usually think of perception as an interpersonally significant activity. That is, while we certainly recognize that other people are included in the world we perceive, we do not tend to think of them as included in the act of perception itself. Indeed, we tend to distinguish our perception of the world from our relationships with other people. We often assume that perception is effected individually and that our perceptions, unlike attitudes such as trust that are generated in our interactions with other people, offer us a consistent and impartial representation of the world. Yet, I will argue, such a sharp separation between our perception of the world and our relationships with other people is not tenable. Our relationships with other people deeply inform our perception of the world and, indeed, constitute our perception of the world as a shared world. In short, we are *always* dealing with other people, whether we notice this explicitly or not.

To grasp the role of others in our experience, we must first get clear on *how* we experience others: it is this distinctive character of our awareness of others that we will investigate. To do this, though, we must first address the very notion of an "awareness of others," for this notion seems to harbor within it a contradiction: another person is not a simple object of perception like a tree or a book, for another person is precisely an *other*—an individual who, in her own nature, holds her distinctive reality apart from herself. For that reason, though, others are an epistemological mystery, for the very nature of being another *subject* seems to entail an inherent privacy to what it is to be that person—an inherently "inner" life—and thus something that, by definition, would escape our ("external") perception. Indeed, it has often seemed to theorists that others cannot be known, hence the so-called "problem of other minds": from the outside, it seems, we could never get to the inside. On the face of it, then, "awareness of others" does not even seem possible.

In *Being and Time*, however, the twentieth-century phenomenologist Martin Heidegger argues, on the contrary, that our experience—indeed, our very *being*—is always a being-with-others. Being-with is not, in other words, characteristic of some of our experiences: those, for example, in which we are explicitly aware of another person or persons. Rather, being-with is characteristic of all our experiences. Thus, I can, for example, be alone and yet feel very connected with others, and I can be surrounded by others and yet feel lonely. Regardless of whether other people are directly present to us, other people are indirectly present to us in the meaning that whatever is directly present to us has. The way I dress myself in the morning, the way I walk down the street, and the way I eat my lunch reflect my implicit awareness of others. When we turn to our own experience, it is clear that others are in fact always present to us; indeed, the very fact that the "problem of other minds" makes sense to us indicates that we clearly live with a sense of what an "other mind" would be.

This, then, will be our task: to turn to the nature of our experience in order to define more precisely how other people are present in our perceptual life. This is both a theoretical matter—addressing the issue in principle of whether and how awareness of others is possible—and an empirical matter—addressing the concrete, specific ways in which others show up in our experience. What our study will ultimately show is that, far from being a kind of reality inherently excluded from our experience, other people will prove to be right there at the most intimate heart of our experience. Other people, we shall see, shape the very way we have a perceptual life at all.

This work is a study on and within the philosophical tradition of phenomenology. Phenomenology is primarily a philosophical method: the description of experience. This method was introduced by Edmund Husserl in the early twentieth century, as I explain in chapter 1. My work draws on the insights of Husserl—especially his conception of *intentionality*—but it is primarily rooted in the later "existential" phenomenology of Maurice Merleau-Ponty, who took Husserl's philosophical method and developed from it a rich account of the *embodied* character of our experience. In each of my chapters, it is the insights of Merleau-Ponty—primarily from his work, *Phenomenology of Perception* (1945)—that I will explain and that I will use to produce original phenomenological interpretations of our experience of other people. I will also draw quite substantially on the insights of John Russon—and especially his concept of *polytemporality*—whose writings from the early twenty-first century carry forward the phenomenological project introduced by Husserl and Merleau-Ponty into concrete studies of personal and interpersonal life. These three figures—Husserl, Merleau-Ponty, and Russon—offer a progressively deeper grasp of the character and meaning of our experience, especially as it relates to our experience of other people. Specifically, they demonstrate that the explicit "objects" of our experience that we typically imagine to be what our experience is "about" have the meaning that they do because they are contextualized by many layers of bodily and temporal meaning—layers of meaning that are not explicit in our perception. The "description of experience," therefore, is not a simple listing of the obvious features of our experience, but it is a deeply self-critical probing that ultimately cannot be separated from behavioral transformation.

After explaining and defending the revolutionary insights of these figures, I turn this phenomenological method to the core question of the nature of our experience of other people. In chapter 2, Husserl's concept of "pairing" (*Paarung*) provides the basis for understanding the precise nature of our experience of other people. The developments of the implications of this notion in Merleau-Ponty and Russon, however, will take us to the central argumentative thesis of this book: because our self-experience is paired with our experience of others, the perspectives of others shape the very way in which we perceive; consequently, others are not just "contents" of our experience but are also integral to its "form."

The analysis of "pairing" demonstrates that our own experience as perceivers is always shaped by our experience of being perceived by others. The major contribution of my study is the concrete working out of this "shaping," which I carry out in chapters 3 and 4. These chapters are phenomenological analyses of the experiences we have of others where those others are not experienced by us as contents of our experience that could be exchanged for any others; these are experiences, instead, in which *this specific other person* is experienced by us as in some way uniquely essential to us.

Childhood experiences of parents or other caregivers is the subject of chapter 3. Drawing initially on a range of empirical psychological studies of infant-caregiver relations, I show how pairing is operative in these relationships. I then use these analyses to demonstrate the thesis that, because we are essentially paired with specific others, interpersonal trust is the condition of healthy perceptual development.

Adult sexual experience is the subject of chapter 4. Here, I use phenomenological analyses of sexuality initially to demonstrate that what is implicitly at stake in our sexual relationships is the same issue of "being recognized as a subject" that is central both to the general phenomenological account of the experience of others and to the understanding of child-parent pairings. On the basis of this, I argue again that trust is the essential medium of our erotic relationships, relationships that in principle carry an equivalent sort of ethical weight to that of the caregiver relationships studied in chapter 3.

Through these original phenomenological interpretations of childhood and sexuality, I show that there are experiences of other people that are formative of our very existence as subjects. Moreover, these experiences are largely carried out at a nonreflective, bodily level, and it is at that level, too, that they tend to leave their significance. The very meaning of the world of our explicit perception is essentially shaped by this implicit, intersubjective background.

In our everyday life we talk regularly about good and bad behavior and about which political party we endorse. All studies of ethics and politics, from the most everyday to the most theoretical, rest on the presumption of our relations with others; that is, *that* we experience other people is taken for granted as the necessary premise behind any ethical or political reflection. In other words, by the time ethical and political questions are posed, we have already established a meaningful world with others. It is this establishing of a meaningful world with others—the experiential background to our ethics and politics—that is the real subject of this work.

1

Phenomenology

Introduction

What do we perceive? An obvious answer would be that we perceive a specific physical object—for example, this cup. Yet, what if, rather than beginning with this answer, we actually turned to our perceptual experience and tried to describe what we perceive? We might think that we already have a good grasp of our perceptual experience; it is, after all, *our* perceptual experience. We might think, then, that we already know what the results of such a description will be and that there is no need for us to actually give it. Moreover, we might think that since we already know what our experience is like, those who do give a description are unnecessarily complicating what is already evident. The project of phenomenology, the philosophical method pioneered by Husserl, is just such a description of experience and, in fact, such a description, far from being a simple repetition of what is already obvious to us, is in fact a revolutionary transformation within our experience.

Husserl and Intentionality

In what Husserl, in his groundbreaking work *Ideas*, calls our "natural attitude"—the attitude we normally adopt in our everyday life—we take our consciousness of physical objects for granted.[1] We assume that the things we perceive first exist independently of our consciousness of them, and we assume that their existence in themselves explains our awareness of them, their existence "for us." This line of thinking often leads us, then, to think that we are actually conscious of "mental representations"—cognitive constructions we make based on the sensory stimulation produced in us by things in the world. In fact, though, a careful description of our perceptual experience reveals that the things we perceive cannot be equated with such mental representations, objects that are, by definition, distinct from real objects. Though everything we are conscious of is indeed relative to us, inasmuch as it is by definition the object of our experience, everything we are conscious of is not *merely* relative to us. The categories of the "in-itself" and the "for-us" are in fact not mutually exclusive and thus being "for-us" does not necessarily mean being "in our minds" rather than "in the world."

Husserl argues that we must put aside the question of whether the things we perceive correspond to the "reality" that we presume to be independently defined and independently existent and begin, instead, by simply describing the things we perceive. If, for example, I look out the front window of my house, I see my neighbor's house. Yet this is inadequate as a description: I do not simply see my neighbor's house. In fact, I see my neighbor's house *across the street* and *in the midst of some trees*. While I may not usually notice that, in addition to the house, I also see a street and trees, I would certainly be surprised if I looked out my window and saw the house across a river or in the midst of a city. Moreover, I can, upon reflection, realize that while I could see this house in a different place, surrounded by different things—if it were lifted from its foundation and moved to another site—I could never see it in no place, surrounded by nothing.[2] In other words, I cannot see just one thing. If I am seeing one thing, I must be seeing other things as well; I can only see one thing surrounded by other things.

Our description still needs further refinement, however. It is true that I see both the house and the street, but when I am looking at the house across the street I do not see the house *in the same way* that I see the street. The house "stands out," and I see it quite determinately. I barely notice the street and trees, though, and I see them much less determinately. Just as I do not ever see only one thing but, instead, see one thing surrounded by other things, I also do not ever see all things equally determinately or prominently. Instead, I see some things more determinately and more prominently than others.

I am not, however, restricted to seeing the house more determinately than the trees. After all, a branch on one of the trees can suddenly catch my eye, and I can see the tree as determinately as I saw the house before and, simultaneously, see the house as indeterminately as I saw the tree before. When this occurs, I see the tree *as* always having been as I see it now, although in fact it was not fully determinate in my perception prior to my attending to it. In other words, neither the determinateness nor the indeterminateness of the things surrounding the house is permanent. Instead, the indeterminateness is one that can be made more determinate, an indeterminateness that is potentially determinate: I can come to see and, indeed, may already have seen, determinately what I now see indeterminately. Similarly, just as I come to see determinately what I previously saw indeterminately, I come to see indeterminately what I previously saw determinately. This variability in what, within my perception, is determinate and what indeterminate is constitutive of all of my perceptual experience: in short, perception always has a structure of "figure and background." In Husserl's language, we would say that to see one thing, this one thing must have an "outer horizon":[3] it must be surrounded by other things, things that have, he says, a "determinable indeterminateness"—an indeterminateness that *would* become determinate were I to make it the focus of my attention.[4]

We can go still further in describing our experience precisely and accurately. Just as I do not see only my neighbor's house but, instead, see my neighbor's house as a figure against a ground of a street and trees, my seeing of the house itself is also not simple. I never have the whole house in my actual experience; instead, I always see the house from this side or that: in Husserl's language, I see it "in profile" or through an "aspect" (*Abschattung*).[5] Just as we do not typically notice the other things that contextualize our perception of an object, so do we not usually notice that we do not see the whole of the thing we perceive. This recognition that what we perceive is perceived as "in profile" has significant implications.

As I walk around a table, for example, I continue to see *the same* table even as specific parts of the table come into, and then pass out of, view. Similarly, I continue to see the table as having *the same* color, even as certain parts of the table are bathed in light and other parts are hidden in shadow; Husserl writes, "The same color appears 'in' continuous multiplicities of profiles of color [*Farbenabschattungen*]. Something similar holds for other sensuous qualities and also for every spatial shape. The one, same shape (given 'in person' as the same) appears continuously but always 'in a different manner,' always in different profiles of shape [*Gestaltabschattungen*]."[6] Thus, typically, I would say, "I see the house," not, "I see the front of a house," and, indeed, we do perceive the house *as* a whole, even though we only actually perceive a profile. In other words, we precisely see the house—or any object—*as* exceeding our perspective upon it: we see the object *as* something real. If we describe our experience carefully and accurately, we must acknowledge our experience has the form of *presenting* us with real objects, objects we experience *as* exceeding our experience of them.

To be conscious of a thing as in profile is to be conscious of this thing as being irreducible to our consciousness of it. We are conscious of the things we perceive as offering more to consciousness than we are conscious of. This "more" is not, however, another thing beyond the thing that we perceive. Husserl stresses that the things we perceive are not mere signs of a "real" thing that we do not perceive; "The spatial physical thing which we see is, with all its transcendence, still something perceived, given 'in person' in the manner peculiar to consciousness. It is not the case that, in its stead, a picture or sign is given. A picture-consciousness or a sign-consciousness must not be substituted for perception."[7] Instead, this "more" is more of the thing that we already perceive.

That we are conscious of the things we perceive *as* these particular things rather than other particular things entails that, analogously to the way in which the tree and the street are "on the horizon" of the perception of the house, so are the further profiles of the thing "on the horizon" of whatever profile we are actually experiencing. Husserl refers to this horizon of further profiles as the "inner horizon" of a thing.[8] The thing itself, like the world surrounding the house, offers itself to our perception as a "horizon of determinable indeterminateness"[9]; this indeterminateness, Husserl writes,

> necessarily signifies a determinableness which has a rigorously prescribed style. It points ahead to possible perceptual multiplicities which, merging continuously into one another, join together to make up the unity of one perception in which the continuously enduring physical thing is always showing some new "sides" (or else an old "side" as returning) in a new series of profiles [*Abschattungen*]. . . . The indeterminacies become more precisely determined.[10]

The horizons that are constitutive of the object of our perception are thus not further *objects that* we perceive. They are, rather, the *immanent meaning of* all of the things that we perceive. When I look out at the ocean, for example, I do not see the ocean as having a horizon in the way that I see the ocean as being choppy or calm: the perceptual horizon is not one more empirical "attribute" of the ocean. Rather, I see the ocean as having a horizon insofar as I am *implicitly conscious of the ocean as* continuing to exist beyond what I see of it.[11] The house that I perceive, then, is not itself "contained" within my experience of it; it is, rather, the essential meaning that defines all my perspectival experiences of it, a meaning that is precisely given as exceeding the finite terms of those limited experiences.

Like the figure-background structure, the horizon structure is not a contingent feature of some perceptions, but it is the very form of our experience of objects as such: "[I]t is evident and drawn from the essence of spatial physical things . . . that, necessarily a being of that kind can be given in perception only through a profile [*Abschattung*]."[12] Thus, when Husserl describes physical objects as "transcendent"[13] to consciousness, he is not claiming that the things we are conscious of as physical objects first exist independently of our consciousness of them, as we presume in the "natural attitude"; he is rather describing the way in which these things exist *within* our experience.

Consciousness, then, is not a container for a collection of "mental representations." Instead, consciousness is, in Husserl's language, "intentional": it is the very presenting of some defining object; "the word intentionality signifies nothing else than this universal fundamental property of consciousness: to be consciousness *of* something."[14] In the case of perceptual consciousness, the meaning of this defining object is that it exceeds our experience of it.[15] Perceptual consciousness is always "of" a "transcendent" object.[16]

It is by describing what we perceive *as* objects of consciousness that we can recognize that what we perceive are real things rather than mental representations. In the introduction to part 1 of the *Phenomenology of Perception*, Merleau-Ponty writes that "we must come to understand how, paradoxically, there is *for-us* an *in-itself.*"[17] Husserl has shown us that there can be an in-itself that is for-us precisely insofar as our perceptual consciousness is "intentional"—always "of" an object that is given with the meaning that it exceeds our experience of it. To refer to what we perceive as an in-itself for-us is not to fall into contradiction but, instead, to offer a careful description of the "horizon of determinable indeterminateness" that defines perceptual experience. We are conscious of something *as* real, rather than *as*, for example, imagined or illusory, precisely because we are conscious of it *as* present to us in profile.

To be a perceptual consciousness, to be a consciousness that takes the form of a perspective, is to be a consciousness that always tacitly recognizes itself as being *one* of many possible consciousnesses of what we perceive rather than being *the* consciousness of what we perceive. Thus, although what we perceive is always what we are conscious of, this does not preclude us from being conscious of things that exist "in the world" rather than "in our minds." Indeed, it is perceptual consciousness's tacit recognition of itself as a perspective—its tacit recognition of its consciousness of what we perceive as only one way out of many possible ways to be conscious of what we perceive—that insures there is a kind of objectivity within subjectivity. Insofar as we are consciousnesses of objects in profile rather than consciousnesses of objects in full, we are not trapped in our minds with no access to anything beyond our own thoughts or "representations." Instead, we are engaged with a real world that constantly calls on us to perceive it more adequately. As Husserl writes, what we perceive "calls out to us, as it were . . . 'There is still more to see here, turn me so that you can see all my sides, let your gaze run through me, draw closer to me, open me up, divide me up; keep on looking me over again and again, turning me to see all my sides.' "[18] In the experience of the inner and outer horizons of what we perceive, we experience what we perceive as imposing a norm upon us; these horizons "prescribe a rule for the transition to actualizing appearances."[19] In perceptual experience, it is we who answer to the world as much as the world that answers to us. Moreover, not only does what we perceive call on us to experience it more fully, but it also calls on us as *bodies*; it calls on us, that is, in our capacities for moving and grasping.[20] The object of our perception presents us with a sort of norm—a "call" or imperative—and it is a norm that we answer to behaviorally, that is, in a worldly, "embodied" manner and not simply in a "mental," imaginative manner.

Husserl has shown that our experience is a *presentation* of the world, not a *representation*, and thus our experience—the "intentionality" of consciousness—is inherently "objective" rather than "subjective" in that it is always already occupied with a reality that is given as transcending it. At the same time, however, inasmuch as a contribution on our part is involved in perceiving the world adequately, the object of our experience cannot simply be understood as one-sidedly determining our perception. Merleau-Ponty's philosophy is particularly powerful in exploring the nature of this, our contribution to our perceptual experience. In *The Structure of Behavior* and the *Phenomenology of Perception*, Merleau-Ponty argues that perception presents, rather than represents, the world to us.[21] The world we perceive is not the *image* of an already given world, but, at the same time, the world thus perceived is an original and meaningful achievement. In this way, perception is as much *expressive of* a subject as it is *responsive to* an object.[22]

Merleau-Ponty and Embodiment

It is the perceptual subject's existence—*our* existence—as a body that is Merleau-Ponty's primary focus: in the *Phenomenology of Perception*, he writes, "[W]e are in the world through our bodies, and . . . we perceive the world with our bodies."[23] The bodily character of our perception is itself constitutive of the meaning and form of our experienced world. The stairs I perceive outside my office, for example, can only be stairs, can only be a way of entering or exiting the building, for a being who can walk up and down them—a *moving* being.[24] It is not, therefore, because I perceive the stairs that I am able to walk down them; rather, it is because I am able to walk up and down them that I perceive them as stairs. "Stairs" is a possible meaning—a possible *reality*—only for a moving being.

Furthermore, the perception of the stairs as such is itself accomplished *in walking*. As we considered above, it is common for us to imagine perception to be an exclusively sensory, "cognitive" matter. A description of our perception of stairs, however, must acknowledge that it is fundamentally a *practical* rather than a *theoretical* activity. It is something we *do* in and through our motor behavior, rather than being a separate activity of reflective contemplation. The core of this phenomenological insight is found in Heidegger's *Being and Time*.

In *Being and Time*, Heidegger's description of our experience as "being-in-the-world" (*In-der-Welt-sein*) emphasizes that we do not usually experience the things that surround us as a collection of objects that we neutrally observe; rather, we normally experience the things that surround us as the medium and means for the realization of our projects.[25] Such things are experienced as "ready to hand" (*zuhanden*), and our normal engagement with these "ready" things does not require our explicit attention. Thus, to use Heidegger's example, when we are engaging with a hammer *as* a hammer—that is, when we are *using* it—we do not focus on the hammer but, instead, on whatever we are building with the hammer. Precisely because the things with which we are practically engaged do not require our explicit attention, we often overlook our practical engagements with things when we attempt to account for our experience of the world and, instead, focus only our theoretical engagements. In fact, though, Heidegger notices, it is typically only when useful things break down that we experience the things of our everyday, practical environment as "objects": if the head of the hammer falls off in the midst of our hammering, our attention is drawn to the hammer itself; in that case, though, we precisely experience it as broken, which is to say that what was its defining perceptual character has in fact been lost. This is the insight behind Merleau-Ponty's phenomenological description of the embodied character of our perception.

It is in and through our "doing" that we typically grasp the world, and this "doing" is first and foremost a bodily matter. Behavior is perceptive, and this means we live the meanings of our world first as bodily comportments rather than mental ideas.[26] Indeed, it is largely for this reason that the phenomenological description of our experience can be educative and, indeed, transformative: our perception is not first and foremost a matter of theoretical cognition, that is, we are not automatically reflectively cognizant of the perceptual significance that defines our bodily comportment towards the world. As I am writing these words, for example, my feet, legs, and arms are touching the floor, chair, and table, keeping my body upright and stable so that I am able to write. My attention, however, is not on my bodily behavior—not even on my fingers depressing the keys on my keyboard—but on the ideas that are materializing through my typing. Typically, our bodies handle most of the things they interact with so competently that we generally do not explicitly notice these worldly interactions. It is nonetheless true, of course, that it must be *I* who am typing, and thus I am not *unaware* of my body. This inexplicit, lived sense of one's acting body is what Merleau-Ponty refers to as a "body schema" (*le schéma corporel*).[27] When one is acting, one does not have an "objective" *cognition* of the empirical details of one's body, but has, rather, a lived sense of how to deploy it—an implicit sense of one's determinate powers for bodily engagement that are "at the ready," powers that will rise to meet the demands of our projects as the unfolding of those projects call them up, as the sting of the mosquito on my shoulder, for example, calls forth my hand to address it, generally without my even noticing it.[28] In this sense, as Merleau-Ponty writes, "consciousness is originarily not an 'I think that,' but rather an 'I can.'"[29] We are, for the most part, focused on the projects sustained by our bodies rather than on our bodies themselves, and we will very likely not be explicitly aware of the specific movements in and contact with the world that our bodies make as we are carrying out our projects.

Describing this behavioral, perceptual significance that defines our everyday reality but that typically eludes our explicit attention adds a further layer of significance that brings us back to the theme of our initial description of the contextual character of our perception of objects. As was noted above, Heidegger describes our experience as "being-in-the-world." The significance of this description is that we do not first exist in isolation from the world we experience and only subsequently, following explicit deliberation, come into relation with it. Rather, we first exist in relation to the world; we are always already meaningfully engaged with the world. Husserl, defining our consciousness as "intentional," drew our attention to the fact that consciousness does not exist in the abstract, but it is always "of" something. In describing our experience as "being-in-the-world," Heidegger draws our attention to that fact that this "something" with which we are involved is a *world*, that is, the particular object, such as the hammer, with which I am involved is *itself* not a strictly separable thing, but is part of the fabric of a meaningful *situation*.[30]

We noted above that the interruption of our practical engagement with the world makes the "ready" thing with which we were involved—the broken hammer—become objectively obvious to us. Beyond the thing itself, our larger project of practical involvement is made manifest in this interruption. We were not, for example, simply hammering for the sake of pounding nails. We were, instead, hammering in order to repair our front porch, we were repairing our front porch so that we could sit on the porch with friends the next night, and we aim to maintain and pursue those friendships for the sake of living a rich and fulfilling life. Though we often, I think, try to define our practical engagements quite narrowly, our practical engagements are not totally isolated from one another. Smaller projects—like repairing the front porch—contribute to larger projects, and these larger projects ultimately contribute to our overall project of living a meaningful life.[31] We must recognize, therefore, that our behavior, that is to say, our *perception*, is an *existential* activity: it is our way of having a world.[32] In comporting ourselves as we do, we are building a life for ourselves, and it is this life that is the true focus of perception. Thus, for example, in walking down the stairs, I am not just walking down the stairs but also leaving my office in time to make dinner for some friends: the stairs are my route home and my keeping of a commitment.[33] We are invested in what we perceive; it matters to us as our way of making a living or being a friend. In making manifest these deeper layers of our life-projects, the breakdown of the ready thing, then, precisely offers us the opportunity to notice that we did not previously live the world as a neutral collection of objects. This is the point behind Merleau-Ponty's phenomenological analysis of the experience of a "phantom limb."

With the loss of a limb, as with the breakdown of a tool like a hammer, comes a sudden awareness of the limb's contribution to one's way of being-in-the world. In an obvious way, without a leg, I cannot walk, and without a hand, I cannot grab: my capacities for interacting with the world that confronts me are diminished when my body is damaged. The striking phenomenon of the "phantom limb," however, reveals that my bodily capacities are implicated at the even deeper level of *the very constitution of this world*.

"Phantom limb" experience is a well-documented phenomenon in which those who have lost limbs continue to experience feelings *in the* (absent) *limb itself*.[34] Further, this experience defies both physiological and psychological explanations: it cannot be a strictly "subjective," psychological phenomenon because the phantom limb experience can be diminished or eliminated by physiological means (such as cauterization or drugs); it also cannot be a strictly "objective," physiological phenomenon because the experience can be triggered by memories.[35] Rather than these categories that presume the separation of "subjective" and "objective," it is precisely the phenomenological notion of "being-in-the-world," Merleau-Ponty argues, that allows us to understand how the phantom limb experience is possible.[36]

To understand the phantom limb, we must recognize that the amputation is fundamentally the loss of one's former way of being-in-the-world. With the loss of a leg, for example, the world as a domain in which I can walk is lost. Formerly, stairs, for example, as ready means of access to the building, immediately solicited the appropriate climbing behavior from me without my even reflecting upon it: I perceived the stairs, that is, in and as the bodily behavior of using them to enter the building. The experience of the phantom limb is the continuing experience of this solicitation from the world—a world that immediately calls forth from me the behavior of walking—in a situation in which in fact I can no longer walk. Moreover, these stairs were perceived not simply abstractly as "access to a building" but as access, for example, to the kindergarten classroom where I picked up my child at the end of the day or to the laboratory where I was conducting research. The disruption of my existence as a walker, then, is the disruption of my existence as a parent or as a scientist. The smaller project of walking up a set of stairs is inextricable from my larger project of picking up my child from school, and this larger project is inextricable from my even larger project of being an involved parent or a respected scientist. The limb thus draws my life as a whole in its train, and its loss similarly puts that whole into question. My *world*, that is, summons forth from me a body that I no longer have. In the experience of the phantom limb, the amputee's body engages with the world only insofar as it can be lived in terms of the past that existed prior to the amputation. As Maria Talero writes, commenting on Merleau-Ponty's analysis, "If being-in-the-world is the way that we are always situated in a world of bodily projects or engagements, then the phantom limb is like a cut-away window onto this world. The visible limb has been lost, and what stands revealed is that current of meaningful involvement and bodily competence that previously ran through it and that continues to reside in the patient's world."[37] What this means is that the phenomenon of the phantom limb takes advantage of the habitual character of perceptual consciousness's intentional structure.

Each of our perceptual experiences is not disconnected from every other perceptual experience. Each experience is not immediately forgotten such that, with each experience, we encounter an entirely new world for which we must discover an entirely new perspective. Rather, our perception of the world has a certain continuity and stability to it. This continuity and stability, Merleau-Ponty argues, are rooted in our body's habits.

When I, for example, begin learning how to type, I do not immediately perceive the keyboard adequately. Grasping the keyboard will happen as it becomes "ready" for me, which will happen through my learning the bodily behavior of navigating the keys. My fingers, too, though, do not immediately take up the stance that will allow me to experience the keyboard as a tool for writing. To develop this behavioral "perspective," I must *learn* how to interact with the keyboard. I must at first focus intently on the movements my fingers are making and on the keys they are trying to hit, and I must practice this activity repeatedly. Yet, as I practice these movements over and over, my experience changes. Rather than continuing to focus on my fingers' movements and the keyboard, my focus gradually shifts from my fingers to that which I want to write. While learning to type, my fingers' interaction with the keyboard was my project, and I had to pursue this project at the expense of any other project. Once I have learned to type, however, my fingers' interaction with the keyboard, rather than being my project, is, instead, in the service of some other project. I am no longer typing simply for the sake of typing: I am typing in order to write a letter or a book. I can properly type—properly interact with the keyboard—when I have developed the appropriate habit.

Thus, to form a habit is to discover—and then stabilize—a new perspective. Not only does a new habit free us up to perceive something else—if we develop a habit of sitting in a chair, for example, we can, then, read a book while sitting in the chair: a new habit also transforms how one perceives what one perceives. Once I learn to speak German, for example, the trips to Germany that I previously experienced as overwhelming become routine. Likewise, once I have learned to drive, places that I previously could only imagine traveling to become legitimate destinations. Furthermore, this new perspective serves as the foundation upon which yet other perspectives can be developed.

In addition to recognizing perceptual consciousness as embodied, therefore, we must also recognize perceptual consciousness as learned.[38] This learning, however, does not consist of simply perceiving more within an already acquired perspective: it is not just a matter of acquiring "information." Rather, this learning consists of transforming the very form of our engagement with the world. In acquiring a habit, I become *committed* to responding to situations in a specific way. As habitual, perceptual consciousness has an impersonal aspect. Once we have developed a habit, a perspective that once required noticeable effort is achieved with so little notice that we no longer experience it as optional; our perspectives become, in a certain way, beyond our say. Indeed, we may find ourselves taking a certain perspective even as we make a real effort to take a different perspective. Thus, for example, I may find my hand reaching for my phone at dinner even after I have vowed not to check my messages while eating with my family. In acquiring a habit, we give up our immediate, present "control" of our behavior and, instead, give ourselves over to the form of relationship that was cultivated through our past. Our bodies, then, are not wholly absorbed into their present interaction with the world, but they carry within them a past in and through which the meaningful form of our world is fixed.

As habitual, our bodies continue to live in the past and are thus constantly selectively refusing to take up certain aspects of the present;

it is this "habitual body" that, Merleau-Ponty argues, is revealed in the phenomenon of the phantom limb.[39] An amputee can still feel as if she still has all her limbs because, as Talero writes, the "current of meaningful involvement and bodily competence" continues to run through the rest of her body and into the world.[40] She continues to perceive the world in terms of her projects; she continues, for example, to see a cup as graspable, for example, or stairs as navigable. Thus, the phenomenon of the phantom limb is a "breakdown" of the ready world that allows us to see that the very meaning of the world itself is inseparably united with the forms of our bodily involvement with it.

Each of the body's actions aims at a way of life rather than just a particular object. These actions are *existentially* significant; they carry a world with them. Moreover, the body's present mode of being-in-the-world is a continuation of or a deviation from the body's prior mode of being-in-the-world. The body's actions answer to the past and the future just as much as they answer to the present; they tacitly remember previous experience and anticipate further experience.[41] To give an adequate description of our experience, then, we cannot only describe the things that are our focus. We must also describe the world in which it is these things, rather than others, that are our focus and in which these things assume their specific meaning. Whatever specific meaning things have for us arise within a larger context of meaning.

Russon and Polytemporality

In *Bearing Witness to Epiphany*, Russon draws our attention to this larger context of meaning that informs all experience through a description of musical experience: specifically, he argues that the temporal structure of musical meaning is a powerful analog for the temporal structure of all experiential meaning. His analysis of music draws out the many nonthematic dimensions of experience that must be operative if we are to perceive the present sound—the note—as music. His analysis of these dimensions of musical experience provides a basic "logic" for understanding the larger structure of the world that contextualizes our everyday experiences.

"To receive music," Russon writes, "is to dance. . . . Music calls the body: it stirs the body to move, and it is only in the body's acceptance of this its transfigured status that the music is allowed to be."[42] In this description of musical experience, Russon draws our attention to its propulsive character and to the body's implication in this character. Musical notes call on us to perceive them as music. That is, each note announces itself as in relation—rather than in isolation—from the others; each note announces itself as part of a project—the piece of music—that the other notes are also part of. To experience music, then, is to allow the notes to take us where they are going; it is to follow their lead. As Russon writes, "The music is real, but it cannot exist without the body's acts of preparation and realization. The music depends upon the body to allow it (the music) to be the causal force. Only within the anticipative openness of the body can the music realize its causal primacy, its authority."[43] If we fail to follow the notes' lead, we may experience the notes, but we will not experience the music itself.

Russon refers to this felt momentum of one aspect of experience toward other aspects of experience as "rhythm." All experience, and not merely musical experience, he argues, has rhythm in this broad sense: "It is this way that the body senses as a propulsion to fulfillment in further sense that I will call 'rhythm.'"[44] That is, all experience is defined by temporal relations of expectation and resolution. The experience of pulling my car into the driveway, for example, is both the anticipation of a future experience of unlocking my front door and greeting my dog and a resolution of the past experience of driving down my street.

Russon argues that not only does musical experience draw our attention to the temporal relations of anticipation and fulfillment that are always at play in experience; it also draws our attention to three distinct ways that these relations are enacted in experience. "Our perception of rhythm in the broad sense reveals that our experience is always temporal, that is, it is always structured in terms of past (where we are coming from), present (where we are), and future (where we are going). What melody, harmony and . . . rhythm show us . . . is that this temporality is itself multilayered."[45] Each of these three dimensions of music—melody, harmony, and rhythm—has, he argues, a distinct temporal significance: the temporality of rhythm, Russon argues, is of a "*punctuated repetition*" of sounds, the temporality of melody is of "the unfolding of a *coherent sequentiality*" of sounds, and the temporality of harmony is one of a "*simultaneity of the resounding*" of sounds.[46] Furthermore, each of these distinct temporalities gives music a distinct layer of meaning. The repetitive regularity of the sounds that constitute the rhythm of a piece, Russon writes, has the meaning of a "platform" upon which the sounds that constitute the melody and harmony are "*established* and by which they are *supported*."⁴⁷ The progressive development of the sounds that constitute the melody provides the piece's "narrative."⁴⁸ Finally, the resonance of the sounds that constitute the harmony provides the piece's "character."⁴⁹ All experience, and not simply musical experience, Russon argues, is defined by the distinct and yet interrelated temporalities of melody, rhythm, and harmony and by the basic meanings of narrative, platform, and character that these distinct temporalities enact. Let us now explore how this is so.

When I meet a friend for coffee, he and I talk of the events of the day or our plans for the summer. Though these topics are the explicit focus of our conversation—its "melody"—there is a deeper sense in which our conversation is "about" our continuing friendship; though we do not explicitly talk about this topic, it is the reason for our getting together, and it provides the essential context for our conversation and, indeed, the fundamental tone—the warm, comfortable, "friendly" tone—of our exchange.⁵⁰ In this sense, then, our friendship is the "harmony" of our conversation, a harmony without which it would not make sense for us to have the conversation we are having. Further, there is a familiar rhythm to our ongoing conversational pattern, such that, for example, we meet every Monday or whenever he is in town. This regularity is the reassuring "rhythm" of our friendship, and our specific conversation will resonate with this rhythmic meaning either by reproducing it comfortably, or by having to address a gap that has emerged between us because it is the first meeting after an unexplained hiatus, or by suggesting something exciting by being a meeting that is coming up more quickly than our meetings normally do. And, indeed, even within my friend's conversation, we can see a "logic"—a "polytemporality"—of melody, harmony, and rhythm.⁵¹ My friend begins talking, and each word he speaks, like each sound in the melody of a piece of music, announces itself as carrying forward something that was begun by previous words and that will continue in future words. He is telling me a story, for example, or making an argument. Like a melody, then, my friend's ongoing interaction with me has a temporality of sequential development. Just as a melody can be direct or meandering, so, too, can my friend's conversation: he may stay on topic or make frequent digressions. Yet in addition to the temporality of melody, my friend's words also have the temporality of rhythm. My friend may be a plodding or a hurried speaker. He may deliver his words in short bursts followed by long pauses or in a consistently flowing stream. Again, the very meaning of the "melody" of his speech will be shaped by this rhythmic meaning: it will be my familiarity with his characteristic rhythm that allows me to grasp the emotional tone of his speech, and whether or not he does in fact repeat this characteristic rhythm will again be highly significant for grasping the sense of his communication. My friend's words, too, are contextualized not only by other words, but also by the facial expressions and gestures that are simultaneous with his words. These facial expressions and gestures resonate with—"harmonize"—my friend's words and give my experience of him its specific character. Words that, when resonating with a smile, will be experienced as friendly will, when resonating with a stern look, be experienced as hostile. Grasping the sense of my interaction with my friend implicitly depends upon my familiarity with his rhythmic style and my attunement to the sense of his body language, and not just upon my correctly ascertaining the discrete meaning of the single words he is presently speaking. In both the broad structure of our friendship, then, and in the internal structure of my friend's speaking, we can see the way that the meaning of our conversation is simultaneously a matter of melody, harmony, and rhythm.

Beyond thinking about an isolated experience like a conversation in terms of melody, harmony, and rhythm, we can also think about the whole of a person's experience in these terms. Whatever experiences she has, a person is herself a living being who, for example, is innately sensitive to natural cycles like "day and night, hunger and drowsiness, the seasons, menstruation, and sexual arousal."[52] She acts, for example, as someone who regularly needs to eat and sleep, and these recurring demands are a meaningful rhythm that is ongoingly definitive of her experience as a whole. In addition to being a living being who answers to the cycles of nature, she is also someone who, in developing certain habits rather than others, has acquired a specific character, and this, too, is formative of the sense of the things she experiences. She acts, for example, as someone for whom honesty with others comes easily or with great difficulty. Her character, which resonates in all her actions even as it is not generally her focus, is the harmony of her experience. Whatever more specific activities occur within her life—experiences like the conversation of our example, with its own intrinsic harmonies and rhythms—these experiences will themselves all be contextualized by these more fundamental structures of rhythm and harmony—"platform" and "character"—that define the *world* of the individual person as such.[53]

Our experience is never, in other words, reducible simply to the specific things or people of which we are explicitly aware. The goings on of these specific things or people do indeed form the melody of our experience, but their significance is always embedded in the more basic form—the rhythm and the harmony—of our experience that is projected by our own natural and habitual character. The relations of anticipation and resolution that are enacted in the activities we explicitly plan for ourselves always exist along with, and draw their power and significance from, more deeply embedded relations of anticipation and resolution that are enacted in the harmony and rhythm of our experience. The sense, for example, of your request that I help you with an errand will be quite different for me if I experience it in light of the exuberance of the start of my day rather than in light of the exhaustion of the end of my day; and again, how I feel that that request calls upon me "to dance," as Russon puts it, will be quite different if I am a person of fundamentally honest or fundamentally dishonest character.

To notice the temporalities of rhythm and harmony that operate within our experience is to notice that the present meanings of the specific people or things that we focus upon are not simply self-defined, but they have their sense given, rather, by their placement within the meaningful context that is our way of having a world. Revising this sense of the meaning of the object of our experience, however, further entails a revision of our sense of ourselves: we typically understand our own activities in terms of the immediate sense of our particular object, not recognizing how much the deeper structures of our experience are simultaneously shaping the meaning of that thing and our behavior toward it. Consequently, our own explicit sense of what we are doing is typically an insufficient grasp of the real structures and motivations that are formative of and operative in our experience. We are not, Russon argues, the "self-possessed intellects . . . who set explicit goals for ourselves that we then accomplish in the world through executing plans through utilizing our bodies upon the world" that we typically take ourselves to be.[54] This "intellectual" model of the person should be replaced with a model of "'musical' subjectivity" that recognizes that "the attitude of giving oneself over to the guiding force of rhythmic epiphany is more basic than the attitude of self-conscious, goal-directed manipulation of limbs and world."[55] The disparity in perspective between a father and a son with whom I am familiar is helpful for illuminating how the unreflective experience of a "world" shapes our present perspective—both cognitively and behaviorally—in ways we do not immediately avow.

The father is a man who grew up in Italy during World War II. Food and other supplies were scarce, and meeting the family's basic needs required everyone in the family, including the children, to work. He had little time to play; weekends and holidays were lived, just like any other day, under the unrelenting pressure to meet the family's basic needs. Several homes in his town were damaged by bombs, and he watched as the families that lived in these homes struggled to repair them. Several years into the war, Nazi soldiers marched into his town and forced many of its male inhabitants, including his father, to join them as they continued their campaign south. His family did not know where his father was, or even if he was alive, until his father returned home several months later. Though his father's absence was deeply upsetting, the precariousness of their situation gave them little chance to acknowledge its emotional toll; his family had to throw themselves even more intensely into their work.

This man's childhood world was one of insecurity and deprivation, and though he now remembers few explicit details about his childhood, it is this *world* that he continues to live as the rhythm and harmony of his present experiences. His relentless work schedule provides the established platform for his present experience, and his habitual preoccupation with further increasing his family's material wealth, coupled with his habitual obliviousness to the physical and emotional toll that this preoccupation takes on him and his family, provides the qualitative character of his present experience. He approached his education as a means of acquiring a well-paying job, and he continues to make decisions about his work based on how much money he will be able to earn: to him, it seemed *obvious* that this was the necessary approach. He also *takes it for granted* that he will find his work uninteresting and tedious, and he is correspondingly unsympathetic to others' experiences of distress or illness, expecting that they, like he, will prioritize continuing to work above all else. In particular, he was appalled by his son's decision to give up a well-paying job in order to pursue his musical interests. He views his son's behavior as placing not just his son, but the entire family, at risk; not only will his son no longer be contributing monetarily to his family, but his son also may very well now require his father's financial support. He considers his son to be lazy and selfish for putting his family in this position, and he responds to his son's decision as an assault on the family.

His son, on the other hand, considers his father to be cruel and insensitive. His childhood, unlike his father's, was one of security, and his lived experience of the world is as basically supportive. He feels no need to constantly prepare for the possibility of economic hardship. He experiences his current office job as an unacceptable distraction from the true focus of his life, and he is confident that he can, if necessary, find another well-paying job in the future. He cannot understand why his father would want him to pursue work he has no real interest in, and he is deeply upset by his father's dismissive attitude toward his musical pursuits.

What is salient in the difference between the perspectives of father and son here is what they take for granted—what they take to be *obvious*.[56] For the father, it is not an explicit focus of his experience but the assumed context of all his perception that "one must work"; for the son, it is not an explicit focus of his experience but the assumed context of all his perception that "one should cultivate one's interests." The *worlds* of father and son are thus structured around orienting principles that are fundamentally different, and these different principles show themselves in the *rhythm* of everyday living that allows them to feel comfortable and in the *harmony* of daily life that is the defining projects that give their daily affairs meaning and purpose. The father feels validated by the rhythm of the alternating struggle of merely instrumental work and the rewarding satisfaction of enjoying the material flourishing of his family, and his particular actions are harmonized by the projects, carried out over years, of progressively improving the social and financial position of his family. The son, on the contrary, feels validated when he can live with the rhythm of unfettered creativity, working at his own pace at developing his music, and his particular actions are harmonized by the gradual unfolding of the various artistic projects that collectively work towards his becoming an independently successful musician. The same set of actions, then, appear quite differently to father and son: the father's actions that seem to himself to be obviously proper and successful seem to the son to be oppressive both to the father himself and to others, whereas the son's actions that seem to himself to be obvious experiences of flourishing seem to the father to be trivial, self-indulgent, and wasteful. We began our study of phenomenology by reflecting on the basic difference between the figure and the background in our perceptual experience; using, now, Russon's notion of the "musical polytemporality" of experience, we can see, in this conflict between father and son, how rich, deep and complex this perceptual background is.

The rhythmic and harmonic dimensions of our experience mean that we encounter things with a certain already established momentum that makes it far more likely that we experience these things in certain ways rather than others. Insofar as the platform and character of my experience inform the meaning of all those things that I explicitly attend to, I often do not realize that these things could have a different meaning. To experience things differently, then, I must first realize that my perception is not simply a neutral observation of "how things obviously are," but is instead an interpretation—a perspective that is deeply shaped by habitual expectations. Enacting such a change in perception may, however, be more difficult than we would expect, and I will focus shortly on why this is the case.

The rhythmic and harmonic dimensions of our experience usually define the perspective through which the things that are our focus take on their significance rather than being themselves the focus of our experience. The rhythm of work and success and the harmony of the project of furthering his family's economic and cultural advancement are, as we noted above, taken by the father in our example to be *obvious* structures of meaningful experience and thus are not noticed by him as optional features of perception—certainly not as meaningful components of experience that *he* is contributing. Similarly, the rhythm of self-defined activity and the harmony of creative self-development are taken by the son to be *obvious* structures of meaningful life rather than appearing to him as simply his own preferences. For either of these two individuals, to recognize these features as optional would be to recognize them as dubitable, as matters of opinion, whereas *for* the father and *for* the son they seem simply to be matters of fact. To recognize these deep rhythms and harmonies of our experience, then, is not a simple matter of observation, but involves adopting a significantly self-critical attitude.

While these dimensions of our perspective are not generally something we are aware of, we can become aware of them and, because they are rooted in our own habits, we can change them. We can imagine that this father or this son might want to change his way of acting in order to be more accommodating to the wishes of the other. Yet even as one explicitly wants to change this or that behavior, it can prove very difficult to do so. This is because the real issue is not found in the simple behavior that is the explicit focus of our attention, but it is found in the orienting rhythms and harmonies that give that behavior meaning. To make a change, we will have to acknowledge that the rhythmic and harmonic dimensions of our experience, though they allowed us to inhabit the world comfortably in the past, are now a source of discomfort. Though the habits we have developed were important ways of building a life for ourselves, they now impede, rather than support, our continuing development. These habits, though, are not themselves matters that one finds optional, but they have rather become the very fabric of how one finds things meaningful. Consequently, to change my behavior, I must transform the way that I inhabit the world.

In a very deep way, then, we can now see the significance of the idea that the description of our experience—"phenomenology"—is not a simple or an obvious matter: to grasp what is actually happening in our experience requires us to recognize our deeply submerged prejudices, commitments, and expectations, deeply submerged structures that have precisely become the structure—the "platform and character"—upon which *the meaningfulness of our lives* rests.

Conclusion

Throughout this chapter, we have been reflecting on phenomenology as the project of describing our experience. What we have seen, in progressively deeper and richer ways, is that our experience fundamentally has a "figure-background" structure and that to describe our experience well, therefore, requires that we make explicit the otherwise nonreflective "background" elements that are always formative of our experience and that determine the founding parameters—the "platform" and "character," as Russon puts it—of the more focal meanings of our experience. What we will now investigate more directly is our experience of other people—in their role as focal objects of our experience, but also in their role in the formative backgrounds of experience.

2

The Phenomenological Approach to the Experience of Others

Introduction

Traditionally, it has seemed to many philosophical thinkers that we can never directly experience other people, and thus that we can never be certain that other people do, in fact, exist. What is definitive of a person is that she is a subject rather than an object. Another person, that is, has the same sort of consciousness of things that we ourselves have. The very nature of our consciousness, though, as we have seen in chapter 1, is that we are never reducible to the things of which we are aware, as those things would appear objectively to another observer; on the contrary, we are always taking things up in a *meaningful* way, a contextualized way that reflects the distinct character of our own *perspective*. Because I am able to determine for myself what I will pay attention to—what will be figure and what background in my experience—my experience, my subjectivity, can never be simply reduced to anything observable "from the outside."[1] "My point of view," then, can never be the object of the direct experience of another person. Thus, the very fact that we experience, the very fact that we are conscious, would seem to preclude any direct experience by one person of another person as such.

This problem, often referred to as the problem of other minds, is articulated quite clearly by René Descartes in the second of his *Meditations on First Philosophy*, when he asks how he can be sure that the beings he sees on the street are actually people and not just very complex machines. Although some recent scholarship on Descartes argues that Descartes was not, in fact, a "Cartesian Dualist" and that he did not think that knowledge of other minds was a problem, the idea that we cannot directly experience other people—that is, that we cannot directly experience other minds—continues to dominate much research in psychology and the cognitive sciences.[2] As the psychologist Vasudevi Reddy, whose work I will draw on elsewhere in this chapter and the next, writes,

> It is almost the first principle of student training manuals on how to observe behavior that description must be separated from interpretation—in other words, that physical movement is separate from its psychological meaning. The behavior of the body is seen as transparent to the observer, while its "mental" or "intentional" meaning is seen as opaque and only accessible to interpretation and inference. . . . A belief in the deep unreliability of the connection between behavior and mind is often asserted as strongly as a religious tenet.[3]

Our own sense of the nature of experience thus makes it seem intuitively natural to deny our knowledge of other minds.

Now, if it were true that we could never directly experience other people, then our sense that the human bodies we encounter do have minds would have to be a belief that develops only after extensive experience of their behavior. Starting from the discovery that we who are conscious of objects are also objects of consciousness—starting, that is, from the discovery that our mental activities are correlated with our behavior—we would have to then come to the conclusion that the other human bodies of which we are conscious would themselves also have to be conscious. This assumption is prevalent in much psychological theory, and, very generally, psychologists commonly conceive of this development as occurring in one of two ways: either infants reason from their own first-person experience or they reason from third-person observation.[4] The first, often referred to as "simulation theory," posits that when infants encounter another human body behaving a particular way, they simulate what they would have in mind if they were in this situation and attribute this experience to the other. The second, often referred to as "theory of mind theory" or "theory-theory," posits that when infants observe the behavior of other human bodies, they develop a hypothesis that such behavior is motivated by something like a mind and then test this hypothesis.[5] In both cases, the experience of other people is indirect; infants—and, by extension, adults—can only, in effect, deduce that the other human bodies they experience are, like them, conscious.[6]

Yet phenomenologists have argued that this account of our experience of other people is simply not adequate. The view that other people can never be experienced directly assumes that the only kind of experience we can have of other human bodies is one in which they appear to us as objects. Husserl, however, in his *Cartesian Meditations*, argues that another kind of experience of other human bodies is possible. Through a careful description of our perceptual experience, we discover that although we can encounter other human bodies as objects—as things of which we are conscious—we can also encounter other human bodies as subjects— as beings who are themselves conscious. Moreover, we discover that we encounter these bodies as perceiving subjects engaged with the natural and cultural world that we, too, can perceive rather than as thinking subjects engaged with ideas that are not immediately accessible to us. Thus, rather than simply being aware that others are perceptive, we can also be aware of others as making specific perceptual sense of their specific physical situation. Husserl refers to the latter relation as a relationship of "pairing" (*Paarung*).[7] In a "pairing," we "live through" or "perceive with" other people; the "object" of our perception is not other people as such but, instead, the surrounding world as perceived by these others. In order to appreciate Husserl's discussion of our experience of other people as a "pairing," let us make two clarifications that are crucial to the analysis.

First, the question that guides much research on the experience of other people is whether other people are experienced as having minds. Yet when we focus on other people as having minds, we tend, I think, to focus on acts of thought such as remembering a past event, imagining a future event, or reasoning about the implications of our present activity. Yet subjective experience does not only take the form of explicit, self-conscious thought. To be a person is more fundamentally to be perceptive: it is to be listening to a friend's account of her day or watching the road ahead while driving. Unlike thinking, which we tend to understand as directed inward and separated from the physical world, perception is directed outward and engaged with the physical world. Although we may spend large portions of the day lost in thought, we spend all of our day perceiving the natural and cultural world we inhabit. It is such subjective experience in the form of perception that, I will argue, is central to Husserl's account of our experience of other people.

The second point is that, in thinking about perception, we must hold on to the phenomenological insights we studied in chapter 1. We saw in chapter 1 that phenomenologists argue that to conceive of the object of perception as a mental image is to fundamentally distort perceptual experience; the object of perception is not the image of a real object but the real object itself.[8] We must resist, therefore, the temptation to conceive of perception as *re-presenting* the physical world, and should, instead, conceive of perception as *presenting* the physical world. Further, when we cease conceiving of perception as the production of mental images, we should also cease conceiving of perception as a purely mental activity and, instead, recognize that perception is fundamentally embodied. Our bodies are not simply things that we perceive; our bodies are also, and more fundamentally, themselves perceptive. Behavior is not a mechanical activity disconnected from our perception of the world.[9] When we pick up a hammer to pound a nail into a wall, for example, this activity is our perception of the hammer *as* a hammer, as a tool to be grasped firmly and pounded against nails rather than, for example, as a piece of art to be held gently and simply admired. Our behavior engages the world we perceive as, to use Heidegger's term, a "workshop" (*Werkstatt*) for our current projects, projects in which things matter to us in specific ways and in which certain things matter to us more than others.[10] The intentional structure of subjective experience articulated by Husserl is, in the case of perceptual experience, a bodily or motor intentionality.[11] Rather than distinguishing between our perception of the natural and cultural world and our behavior, then, we must understand our behavior—our practical, bodily activity—as perceptive, as the very enactment of our "subjectivity."

Beginning, then, by focusing on perceiving rather than thinking and by understanding perception phenomenologically as an act that is creative and embodied rather than duplicative and disembodied, let us turn to Husserl.

Husserl and the "Pairing" Relation

In the fifth of his *Cartesian Meditations*, Husserl begins by describing the experience of another person in the following way: "I am here somatically, the center of a primordial 'world' oriented around me. Consequently my entire primordial ownness . . . has the content of the Here. . . . [and] accordingly, not the content belonging to that definite There. Each of these contents excludes the other."[12] In his description of our encounter with another human body as a "There" relative to a "Here" that it is somatically, then, Husserl begins by focusing on an experience of another human body that is premised on the position of one's own body.[13] In other words, Husserl focuses on an experience of *actually perceiving*—rather than imagining or remembering—another human body. The experience of perceiving—in contrast to the experience of imagining or remembering—is inseparable from the body's position. When we perceive, there are, for whatever specific things we perceive, always also specific other things that we do not perceive. We can only see, for example, what is in front of our eyes, and we can only hear what is within the range of our ears. If one's body were positioned differently, then, one would encounter the other human body differently or perhaps not at all.

Husserl's description starts, in other words, from the place where the problem of other minds arises. We can experience another human body as a thing that appears to us, as, to use Husserl's words, "that definite There." Yet in being perceived merely in this way, that other human body is not experienced *as* another person. Insofar as another human body is perceived merely as a thing in the world, as part of the content of the experience from our "Here," we do not experience this body as itself experiencing things, as its own "Here" with its own content; in Husserl's words, the content belonging to the "definite There" is excluded. The simple recognition of another body "there" is not, however, where Husserl's description ends:

> But, since the other body there enters into a pairing association with my body here and, being given perceptually, becomes the core of an appresentation, the core of my experience of a co-existing ego, that ego, according to the whole sense-giving course of the association, must be appresented as an ego now coexisting in the mode There, "such as I should be if I were there."[14]

In experiencing the body there, the other as a perspective is "appresented," in Husserl's language.[15] What he means by this is that, within the very perception of the body we are motivated to recognize something that cannot itself be "simply there," cannot be simply "present." In other words, Husserl is claiming that an accurate phenomenological description of the form that our experiences take reveals that, when we experience another human body, instead of experiencing it only as the objective thing that we perceive, we also experience it as itself perceiving things. The other human body is not just situated indifferently in the world that is oriented around me; this other human body is its own center of a world oriented around it. As Husserl writes, another human body may be a "There 'such as I should be if I were there'" instead of merely a "There." When we encounter another human body, we do not experience this body at its surface, so to speak. That is, the particular parts of another human body that we encounter need not be our sole—or even our primary—focus. Rather, when we encounter another human body, we can, in a sense, experience this body from within; the other human body as a body is not itself the figure of our perception but is instead the context that allows something else to be perceived. Specifically, *through* our perception of that body, we can experience *the world as it is oriented around* this other human body rather than as it is oriented around our own body.

This theme of "orientation" is itself worthy of further discussion. We tend to think of orientation in terms of objective distances like feet and inches and cardinal directions. Phenomenologically speaking, though, this is a very impoverished sense of orientation. To be oriented is not simply to know where one is on a map but to be comfortably navigating the world. A richer understanding of orientation, in other words, recognizes our experience of the world as a "workshop" for our projects rather than as a neutral collection of objects that we dispassionately survey. Orientation, in this richer sense, does not merely reflect our objective spatial position;[16] it reflects our ability to be at home in the world around us and to carry out the projects that are meaningful for us.[17]

In other words, the terms that we often use to describe the spatial relations between things are not adequate to describing *our* spatial relations to things. As Heidegger writes in *Being and Time*, "The primary and even exclusive orientation toward remoteness as measured distances obscures the primordial spatiality of being-in. What is supposedly 'nearest' is by no means that which has the smallest distance 'from us.' What is 'near' [*Nächste*] lies in that which is in the circle of an average reach, grasp and look."[18] Standing on the south rim of the Grand Canyon, for example, I do not first and foremost experience the spatial relation between me and the north rim as an objective distance, as a matter of several miles. Instead, I experience the north rim as extremely remote; indeed, I experience it as far more remote than my home in Flagstaff, even as Flagstaff is many more miles away than the north rim. The remoteness of the north rim, rather than being a matter of objective distance, is, instead, a matter of its inaccessibility to me. Such experiences of remoteness, and related experiences of nearness, reveal that our spatial relations to things are fundamentally defined by the practical meanings these things have for us. Merleau-Ponty describes this space defined by our practical relations to things as "lived space"[19]; "Beyond the physical or geometrical distance existing between me and all things, a lived distance links me to things that count and exist for me, and links them to each other. At each moment, this distance measures the 'scope' of my life."[20]

Phenomenological description reminds us that, when we behave, we do not typically perceive our own behavior, but, instead, perceive the meaningful world this behavior enacts. Analogously, it is more primary for us to perceive the meaningful world enacted by another human body's behavior rather than just the behavior itself. We perceive things as oriented around another human body rather than as simply "surrounding" it. We see someone *as* hurrying to cross the street ahead of the traffic, for example, and not simply as a body meaninglessly traveling through surroundings to which it is insensitive. We see this human body *as* engaged in its own specific project, and thus we see it as wandering around lost or as knowing where it is going. Moreover, if this human body should suddenly deviate from its path, we will look around to discover the obstacle that it was avoiding; that is, we already see the behavior in terms of its meaningful, intended object, in terms of the world it projects.

With this description of our experience of other human bodies, then, Husserl argues that our relation to these bodies is not restricted to confronting them as they are objectively perceived; there is a second kind of relation that we can have to other human bodies, which Husserl refers to as a "pairing."[21] In a "pairing," our experience does not begin from our own bodies and end at the other's body. Instead, our experience begins from our own bodies, extends into the other's body, and ends in a world beyond us both.[22] In a "pairing," another human body gives me access to a meaningful world that it "appresents," rather than standing in the way of that access.[23] And in a "pairing," we "live through" or "perceive with" another human body and find ourselves in a world as perceived by the other rather than simply by us.

Husserl's phenomenological description of our experience of "pairing" with others thus challenges both the "simulation theory" and the "theory theory" approaches to the "problem of other minds." The pairing relation Husserl describes is not experienced as the result of an attributional process: we do not experience the world as oriented around us and then *think about* how it might be oriented differently around another human body. Rather, we immediately experience the world *as* oriented around others. When we see a young child's hand moving in the vicinity of an open kitchen cabinet, for example, we see the child *as* reaching for a bowl, and immediately we see this bowl as out of the child's reach and step in to help.[24] We may, of course, be wrong about the experience we perceive another person as having. And the other person may, indeed, be having thoughts that are distinct from what she or he perceives; I can, for example, be walking to school while thinking about what I am going to have for dinner this evening. Nonetheless, we do experience other human bodies as perceptive, and any mistakes we make about what another perceives are only revealed through further perception.[25] Husserl's phenomenological description thus denies the very premise on which the "problem of other minds" depends.

Merleau-Ponty on the Perception of Others

In his phenomenological description of our experience of other people, Merleau-Ponty further develops the idea that our perception of others is not primarily a cognitive theoretical operation, but is, instead, a practical bodily matter.[26] In other words, it is precisely *our bodies* that we experience as paired with the bodies of others; "just as the parts of my body together form a system, the other's body and my own are a single whole, two sides of a single phenomenon."[27] I will refer to this self-experience of my body as involved with the body of another as a "shared body schema."

We introduced Merleau-Ponty's conception of the body schema in chapter 1: the body schema is the implicit awareness that we have of the articulate way our bodies are functionally available to us. Rather than primarily knowing our bodies directly as things that we perceive, we primarily know our bodies indirectly as perceptive; that is, we know our bodies implicitly in the possibilities we perceive things as affording for our engagement rather than explicitly as a specific thing that we perceive. I know, for example, how far my hand is from the glass beside me, not because I see the distance in inches between the glass and my hand, but because I see the glass as a glass that I can drink from; I see the glass as *within reach*, and thus my perception of the glass is implicitly my awareness of my own body as grasping. Likewise, I know my body's width is narrower than a doorway, not because I know these widths in inches, but because I see the doorway as a means for me to enter and exit the room. My body's distance from a house, again, is implied in my seeing the house as a regular-sized house rather than as a tiny house. I see the house as inviting a perceptual exploration that a tiny house would not invite; I see the house as that which my eyes have only begun to gear into.[28] In each case, I am aware of my body as my possibility of engagement, and that awareness, rather than being the explicit object of my attention, is implicit in my perception of things.

Like Husserl, Merleau-Ponty further emphasizes that one's body is not simply an isolated individual but is also involved in a world of other bodies, and the tacit awareness of one's own body as perceptive is simultaneously a tacit awareness of others' bodies as perceptive. The body schema, thus, is fundamentally a shared body schema.[29] I perceive things as visible not to me alone but to anyone with seeing eyes, such as when, for example, I perceive certain things as overlooked by others and other things as highly visible to others.[30] The very way my body schema is manifest to me, in other words, already involves its implication in a world with others. Thus, just as we recognize, albeit usually tacitly, the very specific ways in which our perceptual experience is beholden to our bodies, we also recognize the very specific ways in which others' perceptual experience is also beholden to their bodies, and these are not two separate experiences but two facets of the form all of our experience takes. As Merleau-Ponty writes, "There is, between my consciousness and my body such as I live it, between this phenomenal body and the other person's phenomenal body such as I see it from the outside, an internal relation that makes the other person appear as the completion of the system."[31] We perceive the bodies of others as, at a basic level, gearing into the world in the same way that our bodies gear into the world; we perceive their eyes, for example, as sustaining their perceptual consciousness of whatever they are turned toward *as visible* and their ears as sustaining their perceptual consciousness of whatever is within range *as audible*. Even though we cannot experience the precise meanings that the world will have for others' bodies, we can, nonetheless, experience these meanings as grounded in more basic meanings that are shared rather than private.[32]

Of course, we cannot experience others' perceptual experience as we can experience our own.[33] Nonetheless, we experience whatever meanings others do experience as grounded in their bodies' gearing into the same world that our bodies gear into. Our experiences will never be identical, but they are also never completely cut off from one another. The differences between our experiences arise out of a shared experience, so we always have the possibility of drawing on this shared experience to make presently unshared meanings into shared meanings. While our experience can never become another's experience, our experience can become more deeply shared with the experiences of others.

Thus, for example, if we do not find in what we perceive meanings that can account for another's behavior, we can turn to the portion of the world that she is gearing into and work to gear into it in a way that reveals meanings that can account for her behavior. In the *Structure of Behavior*, Merleau-Ponty describes a soccer player's experience of a soccer field. For the player, Merleau-Ponty writes, the soccer field:

> is not an "object," that is, the ideal term which can give rise to an indefinite multiplicity of perspectival views and remain equivalent under its apparent transformations. It is pervaded with lines of force (the "yard lines"; those which demarcate the "penalty area") and articulated in sectors (for example, the "openings" between the adversaries) which call for a certain mode of action and which initiate and guide the action as if the player were unaware of it.[34]

For a person who has never played soccer, however, these lines of force will not yet be perceptible. Thus, for example, if I, having never seen others playing and never having played myself, encounter a soccer game, the players' movements will not make much sense to me.[35] That is, although I recognize the players' movements as perceptive, I am unable to actually perceive their sense. I am unable to perceive their movements as responsive to the lines of force described by Merleau-Ponty, which is to say that I am unable to perceive the activity on the soccer field in its significance for the players. And yet I do not consider this significance that it has for the players to be utterly beyond me. Rather, I consider this significance to be discoverable; I perceive the activity on the field as activity that my body has yet to gear into in the way that the players' bodies do. I perceive the activity on the field as activity that, with practice, I could perceive in the significance it has for the players.[36]

With practice, either as an observer or as a player, I will begin to perceive new possibilities in the activity on the soccer field. I will begin to perceive certain gaps between players as "openings." I will perceive certain gaps between players of the opposing team as the possibility of passing the ball to a teammate or as the possibility of scoring a goal. And in doing so, I will develop a perception of the activity on the field not just in its significance for an isolated body but in its significance for the bodies of teammates and opponents involved in a collective activity. As a player, for example, my perception of whether a ball is within my reach will reflect not only my body but also the bodies of my opponents. A ball that is halfway across the undefended field may be within my reach, while a ball that is just behind me may, given the presence of an opponent, be out of reach. This perception of the ball as within my reach is a perception of what the ball affords me not only in terms of my body's skills of running, kicking, and sliding but also in terms of other bodies' skills of running, kicking, and sliding; it is a perception of the ball as perceived by others as well as me, and as perceived in much the same way by others as by me.

It is this perception of a soccer ball's possibilities for me in terms of its possibilities for others that defines the soccer player. To become capable of playing soccer is to become capable of perceiving the field as jointly, and not just individually, significant. The person who is not able to play soccer perceives the field only in terms of its possibilities for her; she sees the ball as within reach, for example, regardless of the position of other players. The person who is able to play soccer, however, sees the ball as within her reach only by simultaneously seeing it as out of reach of most, if not all, of the other players. She does not perceive the field simply from her point of view; she perceives the field from her teammates' and opponents' points of view as well. She perceives *as* a member of a team rather than simply as an individual.

Our primary way of perceiving the world, Merleau-Ponty argues, is as a participant in a collaborative experience. We begin by perceiving the world as those who have learned to play soccer perceive the soccer field: as places that are lived collaboratively rather than in private. Insofar as the body schema is always first a shared body schema, our inhabitation of the world begins as a co-inhabitation. The meanings the world has for one person begin, therefore, as inextricable from the meanings the world has for others.

The body is a subjectivity to which we, as reflective subjects who make explicitly self-conscious decisions about the meanings we realize, are always indebted. The body commits us to shared meanings that we, in our more explicitly chosen engagements with the world, can transform but can never completely leave behind. We never, therefore, fully and simply coincide with ourselves.[37] Yet, Merleau-Ponty argues, this inability to coincide with ourselves as perceivers is simultaneously an ability to coincide with others as perceivers: "This world can remain undivided between my perception and his, the perceiving self enjoys no particular privilege that renders a perceived self impossible, these two are not *cogitationes* enclosed in their immanence, but beings who are transcended by their world and who, consequently, can surely be transcended by each other."[38] Insofar as perceptual consciousness is accomplished through the body's gearing into the world, and insofar as this gearing into the world can be perceived, one perceptual consciousness is never absolutely hidden from other perceptual consciousnesses. The inability to fully grasp one's own perceptual consciousness is simultaneously an ability to partially grasp others' perceptual consciousness: "[T]hrough phenomenological reflection I find vision to be the gaze gearing into the visible world and this is why another's gaze can exist for me and why that expressive instrument that we call a face can bear an existence just as my existence is borne by the knowing apparatus that is my body."[39] What Merleau-Ponty's description of the shared body schema allows us to see is that in the very motions of our body, we are already responsive to our involvement in a world with others. The experience of other people, in other words, is not one special experience among others, but it is more like the very fabric of our enactment of our own bodily life. This theme of the bodily enactment of our involvement with others is, again, powerfully developed in Russon's account of neurosis.

Russon and the Others within Our Own Bodies

In the previous chapter, we noted the ways in which Russon's description of our experience in terms of the "polytemporality" of melody, harmony, and rhythm drew our attention to the inherent complexity of our experience. Every experience, beyond being an experience of a specific thing or things, is also the experience of a world; every experience has an implicit rhythmic dimension and an implicit harmonic dimension as well as an explicit melodic dimension. I want now to return to Russon's description of our experience in terms of harmony, in light of this chapter's discussion of our experience as a fundamentally interpersonal achievement. As I have argued in this chapter, our world is a world, not just of things, but also of other people; to use Heidegger's terms, our being-in-the-world is always simultaneously a being-with others (*Mitsein*).[40] Russon's discussion of harmony is especially rich for exploring this intersubjective dimension of our experience. More specifically, Russon shows that the significant people with whom we are involved in our lives function more as aspects of the *form* of our perception than as its contents or objects.

The harmonic dimension of my experience, Russon writes, consists of the projects and practices that "are not so much individual actions I undertake as they are ways of living. They are the general structuring contexts to which I become habituated."[41] We can now notice that our relations with other people can be some of the most significant of these projects and practices. One's relation to a spouse, children, or parents, like one's relation to a job or a political cause, can become a settled matter that no longer demands one's explicit attention. My adult relation to my elderly parents as their caregiver, for example, may be habitual rather than a topic of ongoing thought: although when I first began caring for my elderly parents this relation was at issue for me and for them, we now take my daily presence in their life and their daily presence in mine for granted. This relation has thus now become a *context from which* the specific activities about which I do think and to which I do give my explicit attention draw their meaning. Thus, even when my experience is focused on things, other people are implicated in this experience. My experience of the dishes in my parents' sink as needing to be washed, for example, is a "melodic" matter, but it makes sense, and it only makes sense, because it is situated in this context of my relationship to my parents as their caregiver; although my parents are not the explicit focus of my attention, my experience of them is nonetheless there in this experience, but it is there as the "harmony," the essential background structure within and against which my melodic action is meaningful. Even when I am not directly interacting with other people, then, my relations with other people are at issue, and my habits with respect to things are simultaneously my habits with respect to people.[42]

Furthermore, we can now notice that our relations with particular people may be so habituated that they structure all of our relations with others. A child's relationship with his mother, for example, may have been quite troubled in that she was largely indifferent to the child's interests and concerns, and when she did pay attention to him, it was primarily to criticize him harshly. Consequently, the child may have come to avoid interacting with his mother and, when they did interact, to become outraged and storm off at the first sign that she was going to criticize him. By developing core habits of interpersonal interaction in such a formative environment, the persistence of those habits means that, even if he now has little direct contact with his mother, she is still present indirectly in how he handles situations of conflict: even when his mother is not present, he continues to live the world as if its possibilities for him were defined by their "pairing." Thus, it may be the case that he is often withdrawn in social situations, and he does not particularly enjoy meeting new people, moreover experiencing even the slightest discord in his relations with others as portending an onslaught of cruel remarks. In other words, his relation with his mother continues to set the terms by which his relations with other people develop, and, unfortunately, these terms primarily stifle, rather than nurture, these relations. In this sense, his troubled relationship with his mother becomes the continuing "harmony" of his interpersonal affairs, even if explicitly—"melodically"—he takes himself to have distanced himself from her.

This structure of a persisting habit of managing interpersonal relationships that is out of keeping with the demands of one's present life is, Russon argues, the essential meaning of the phenomenon of "neurosis." We often think of normal behavior as behavior that is under our self-conscious control and of neurotic behavior as behavior that is, by contrast, compulsive. This description is reasonable as a rough-and-ready identification of the phenomenon, but it is not ultimately sufficient; indeed, in particular, it does not allow us to understand either form of behavior—the normal or the neurotic. Russon begins by arguing that this ideal of normalcy—the ideal of complete control over one's emotions and actions—itself reflects a "neurotic" compulsion for denying those dimensions of our existence that we cannot control.[43] Rather than assuming that individuals possess a "free will" that operates independently of our embodiment (a version of the dualism of "mind" and "body" that we have previously rejected), we should recognize instead that developing a sense of agency—of self-responsibility in shaping our actions and our lives—is something that happens by degrees within a context of habitual and nonreflective behavior.[44] What defines neurotic behavior is not our inability to control this behavior—for in some way this will always be constitutive of any and all behavior at all levels—but, instead, the incompatibility of this behavior with our other behaviors. As Russon writes, "it is always a human situation—and not a normal ego—that is neurotic. The neuroses are the ways in which a multiply figured situation of contact is at odds with itself, such that its inherent trajectory toward freedom is inhibited by its habitual realization of its potentiality."[45] Indeed, "mental illness" generally should not be understood on the model of a "disease" of the "mind," but it should be understood as problems rooted in our habituation to behaviorally navigating the terms—the intersubjective terms—of making sense of our world. Russon writes that "the neuroses mark the inability to coordinate the sectors of habitual life coherently, and psychosis is this same problem now shifted to the core of self-identity."[46] Neurosis is not a problem of weakness of will, but a matter of incompatibility between our habitual patterns of behavior and the demands of our present life.

Neurotic behavior, Russon argues, like any habitual behavior, is the continuation of a past form of interpersonal functioning to which we were introduced and habituated as children by our caregivers.[47] Like any habit, a neurotic habit is a way of experiencing the things of the world as immediately summoning up from oneself a form of responsive behavior. And, like any habit, a neurotic habit is a habit of functioning in a world that is itself inherently intersubjective. Thus, in habitually dealing with the things of the world, one is implicitly dealing with others. Neurotic habits, though, are habits that are fundamentally crippling:

> Neurosis is experiencing a determinate world as the lived demand to behave bodily in ways that cripple a personality in its efforts to realize itself as an integral, coherent agency where the determinacy of the world is itself the congealed memory of patterns of intersubjective recognition—specifically, the memory of family life, that is, the memory of those patterns of recognition through which, and as which, we were made familiar with other people.[48]

In neurotic behavior, a person's caregivers remain present to her even as they are no longer present to her; she remembers them, although this memory of them is enacted as a bodily behavior rather than as an explicit thought about her caregivers; in this case, though, the habitually reenacted intersubjective relationship is itself a troubled one. Russon argues, for example, that a so-called "eating disorder" should properly be understood as a habitual mode of intersubjective behavior, the continuing presence of problematic relations with other people:

> Meals are often charged sites for specifically familial interactions, whether at the breakfast table or at the Thanksgiving dinner. . . . The dinner table can thus be a primary site for the production or reproduction of family order. As a ritual of family membership, eating dinner becomes the space in which one is defined as doing well or poorly as a family member, and, inasmuch as our familial involvements are our primary initiation into the human, intersubjective sphere, eating can become the privileged space for determining whether one is doing well or poorly as a person. . . . At the dinner table, what one is taking in need not be simply food: if the rules of family life are being served, participating in eating can be the way one "takes in" these familial structures. . . . Conflicts within our intersubjective dealings—within our sense of self-identity—can consequently find a welcome site for enactment in the form of neurotic symptoms within these bodily practices . . . that are the . . . memory . . . of our intersubjective dealings.[49]

As children, these behaviors were, at least in some respect, conducive to our continued growth and development: learning to negotiate the family dynamics of the dinner table was learning to participate in family life—an absolutely essential skill for the child. By learning to work within the terms of family life, the child expands the scope of her world and learns to handle this shared world more adeptly. Yet these behaviors that were enabling in the context of dealing with her childhood family are disabling in the context of adult life, for the adult world does not reflect the same idiosyncratic power dynamics that were definitive of her familial relations: "[N]eurotic compulsion is really a habit that was a good habit in a former (formative) context of intersubjective contact but one that is out of joint with the demands of her current situation."[50]

In neurotic behavior, the meanings that the world and others have for a person continues to be determined in concert with the specific people with whom she interacted in the past. Like the phenomenon of the phantom limb analyzed by Merleau-Ponty, neurotic behavior reflects a situation in which the "habit body" and the "body at this moment" are at odds with each other rather than, as is usually the case, in step with each other. Neurosis, in other words, precisely attests to the founding—"harmonizing"—presence of a "world" that is the essential but unnoticed background to the meaningfulness of our behavior: it attests to it, Russon shows, by revealing that the "world" in which one is living is not the "present" world at this moment, but the world of one's formative relations with other people.

The important conclusion of our phenomenological reflection on our experience of other people, then, is the recognition that our relations with other people are not, therefore, just a "content" of our experience: our relations with other people, on the contrary, provide *the very structure* of our experience. Long after we have left our childhood home, for example, we nonetheless continue living with our caregivers in the ways that we eat, sleep, talk, or engage with others sexually. We can now go on to look in more detail at the formative role of other people in our childhood experience and in more adult relationships.

Conclusion

Starting with Husserl, we have seen that we do not begin our experience as isolated egos who then must discover that there are other such egos in the world. On the contrary, our experience begins in a way that is already involved with—already "paired" with—the experience of others. In other words, the isolated ego, rather than the beginning of experience, is, if anything, a form of experiencing that will be developed *within* the more fundamental experience of already being with others. With Merleau-Ponty, we saw this idea further developed in the recognition that the co-experiencing with others is not primarily a matter of reflective thought, but it is a practical, bodily matter: the very way we inhabit our bodies—our "body schema"—is intersubjective, and our behavior ongoingly attests to this sharedness of experience that underlies our sense of reflective individuality. With Russon, finally, we have seen that, precisely because our experience of reflective individuality is premised upon a formative intersubjectivity, we carry "our" others with us as the meaningful context of all our experience, even when we are no longer "actually" engaged with those others. Ultimately, then, our most important and pervasive experience of other people is not as the explicit objects of our experience but as the very form of our experience.

3

The Institution of Interpersonal Life

Introduction

In chapter 2, following Husserl and Merleau-Ponty, we identified the pairing relationship as definitive of our experience of other people, and, drawing upon Russon's analysis of neurosis in particular, we introduced the idea that our pairings are formative of our self-identity in a way that shapes the very form of our perception. We will now look at the pairing relationship—at the intrinsic embeddedness of others in our very bodily comportment—as the founding, formative context of our perceptual life; specifically, we will turn now to the experience of the child. In looking at our *original* experiences of others in this way, we will see that they are also *originative*. This originary intersubjectivity is thus a matter of what Husserl calls *Stiftung*—a matter of the *instituting* of the form of a meaningful world.[1] To pursue our investigation of the intersubjectivity that is constitutive of childhood experience, we will begin with Merleau-Ponty's own remarks on childhood pairing and then look at a variety of contemporary psychological studies that show in some detail the centrality of pairing in childhood experience. We will then turn to Russon's analyses of the formative experiences of such childhood intimacy to see how these founding experiences of others actually provide the very fabric of our experience of ourselves as agents.

Perceiving through Others:
Neonate Imitation, Joint Attention, and Mutual Gaze

Recognizing that our behavior is our perception of a world has consequences for our understanding of other people. As Merleau-Ponty discusses in the *Phenomenology of Perception* and "The Child's Relations with Others," if perception is not the construction of an image within a person's mind but the way this person comports herself toward whatever is around her, then each person's perception of the world is not closed up within herself and unavailable to others' perception. As Merleau-Ponty writes, "But if the other's body is not an object of me, nor my body an object for him, if they are rather behaviors, then the other's positing of me does not reduce me to the status of an object in his field, and my perception of the other does not reduce him to the status of an object in my field."[2] Perception is a public act rather than a private one. Indeed, as we have seen in our discussion of "pairing," it is fundamental to our experience that we perceive—"apperceive," as Husserl might say—others as perceiving and, indeed, our perceiving is (ap)perceived by others as such. Merleau-Ponty discusses such a situation of the perception of perception in the *Phenomenology of Perception*; specifically, he describes how, when he playfully puts the finger of a fifteen-month-old baby between his teeth and pretends to bite, the baby, too, opens his mouth as if, Merleau-Ponty implies, the baby recognizes Merleau-Ponty's intention to bite and is adopting the same intention for himself.

The baby's adoption of Merleau-Ponty's intention cannot, Merleau-Ponty argues, result from the baby's reasoning by analogy. Although Merleau-Ponty's discussion of this reasoning is quite condensed in the *Phenomenology of Perception*, he discusses it more fully in "The Child's Relations with Others."[3] Very briefly, the presumed analogical reasoning would run from (1) the baby's own previous intentions to bite, which are understood as mental events that are not visible to others; to (2) the baby seeing the expressions his own face makes when he intends to bite; to (3) the baby seeing that Merleau-Ponty's facial expressions are similar to his own facial expressions when he, the baby, intends to bite; to (4) the baby ascribing the same intention to bite to Merleau-Ponty. Attributing the baby's adoption of Merleau-Ponty's intention to the baby's reasoning by analogy is, however, untenable because the baby lacks one of the experiences required for such reasoning: he has not seen the expressions his own face makes when he intends to bite. The baby could only have acquired this experience by seeing his own face in a mirror, and the baby, Merleau-Ponty writes, "has hardly even seen his face in a mirror and his teeth do not resemble mine."[4] Moreover, although Merleau-Ponty does not make this point, research suggests that, in any case, infants generally only begin to recognize themselves in a mirror when they are about eighteen months old.⁵ Thus, even if the infant had spent extended time in front of a mirror, these experiences would be unable to furnish the experience needed for such a reasoning by analogy. The baby's adoption of Merleau-Ponty's intention thus attests, Merleau-Ponty argues, to the baby's direct perception of Merleau-Ponty's behavior as perceptive, as intending a meaningful world. Rather than experiencing Merleau-Ponty's facial expressions as strictly physical events and his own intentions to bite as strictly mental events, the baby primarily experiences both as ways of having a world; both are, first and foremost, perceptual structures rather than perceptual contents.⁶

I think that a particularly salient aspect of this situation, although Merleau-Ponty himself does not particularly emphasize it, is his description of his behavior as "playful." Now, we might think of this playful intention or mood as an internal feeling that Merleau-Ponty experiences while he is pretending to bite the baby's finger. Yet, as Heidegger argues in *Being and Time*, our moods are not primarily objects of experience but are, instead, ways of experiencing. "Having a mood," Heidegger writes, "is not itself an inner condition which then reaches forth in an enigmatical way and puts its mark on Things and persons."⁷ Russon makes a similar point:

> To be in a mood is to have objects appear in a certain way. When I am bored, I experience things in the world as dull and uninviting—as boring. It is the things that fail to engage me and offer me exciting routes of action. When I am angry, things are invasive and challenging to my rights and to my personal space. When I am excited, things seem electric, and charged with possibility. When I feel amorous, the world seems enchanted, precious, and welcoming. In each case, to experience the mood—to be "in" the mood—is to have objects in a certain way. The mood is how the world gathers itself up and shows itself to me.⁸

Consequently, rather than understanding Merleau-Ponty's playful mood as simply, or even primarily, a mental event, we must instead recognize it as his way of perceiving the world; it is a *behavior* that is as much expressive of an orientation as it is responsive to a setting. His playful mood is, for example, his focusing on the baby rather than barely noticing him. His playful mood is also his approaching the baby rather than retreating from him and perceiving him as worthy of attention rather than as an unwanted distraction. Finally, his playful mood is in putting the baby's fingers between his (Merleau-Ponty's) teeth rather than just holding them; it is perceiving the baby's fingers as "for pretend biting" rather than "for stroking" or "for examining." In short, Merleau-Ponty's playful mood is not distinct from the world he perceives: to be in a playful mood is to perceive the world as *a place for* play where, among other things, others' fingers are "for pretend biting."[9]

Nonetheless, Merleau-Ponty's behavior, on its own, cannot achieve his perception of the world as a place for play: the coming into being of the play-world requires the collaboration of the baby. However gentle Merleau-Ponty's biting might be, however little pressure his teeth exert on the baby's fingers, the baby need not perceive it as pretend or playful. If the baby does not perceive his own fingers as, in some sense, belonging between Merleau-Ponty's teeth, Merleau-Ponty's behavior will not be truly playful. The "game" exists only if it is "co-constituted."[10]

Now, one might expect, however, that the baby would not perceive his own fingers as belonging between another person's teeth, and thus that he would consider Merleau-Ponty's behavior as threatening and alarming rather than playful. I think, therefore, that it is just as important to notice what Merleau-Ponty does not describe the baby as doing in this situation as it is to notice what he does describe. Specifically, Merleau-Ponty does not describe the baby as objecting to his biting; he does not mention that the baby screams or jerks his hand away. The baby's response suggests, therefore, that he perceives the world as meaningful in that same way that it is meaningful for Merleau-Ponty, namely, as a place for play, as a place where his fingers do belong between Merleau-Ponty's teeth, rather than as it could very well be meaningful for him, as a place where his fingers certainly do not belong between Merleau-Ponty's teeth.

What this description of their playing demonstrates is that, when the baby looks at Merleau-Ponty, he is focused, not on Merleau-Ponty's mouth as simply a perceived object, but on Merleau-Ponty's mouth *as perceptive* of the world as a place for play, as *expressive* of Merleau-Ponty's meaningful perspective. Rather than perceiving Merleau-Ponty's objective body, one could say, the baby perceives *through* it to the intentionality that is "appresented" with it. Thus, in opening his mouth, the baby is not, strictly speaking, "imitating" Merleau-Ponty in the sense of copying an objective motion he sees; he is not simply moving his mouth as Merleau-Ponty moves his mouth. Instead, the baby is participating in

Merleau-Ponty's specific way of perceiving the world; he, too, is perceiving the world as a place for play and pretending to bite.[11]

By perceiving through Merleau-Ponty's body, then, the baby enables them both actually to be playing, and thus the baby's perception, as well as Merleau-Ponty's, must be recognized as inherently collaborative, as "paired." Working together, they achieve a perception of the world that neither could achieve alone. Their interaction, one could say, is the discovery of the world as a landscape of shared possibilities for play. Their hands, faces, and feet take on meanings that are shared between them: fingers are for the other's pretend biting, feet are for the other's tickling, faces are for the call and response of dramatic gesturing, and so forth. If they continue to interact, this landscape will become ever more developed, both in extent and complexity. They may, for example, move beyond each other's bodies as sites for collaborations and take up nearby objects: a couch, for example, may become a place for playing hide and seek, and a spoon, a place for playing "I drop it, and you pick it up." It is a meaningful *world* of playful possibilities that is opened between them.

That infants do behave in the way Merleau-Ponty describes is well supported by contemporary psychological research.[12] Andrew Meltzoff and Keith Moore, for example, have argued that infants as young as a few hours old will open their mouths in response to adults' mouth opening.[13] This research generally refers to the phenomenon described by Merleau-Ponty as "neonate imitation," and thus understands the infant as focusing on the adult's face in order to reproduce the adult's mouth movements for herself. This understanding of the neonate's behavior as specifically "imitative" extends into philosophical evaluations of the research. Shaun Gallagher, for example, while he does argue, "The newborn infant does not attend to the outward appearance of the other, but rather attends to the *action* and *expression* of the other," then continues, "Some time later in development the child comes to interpret the other person's intention through their actions."[14] Thus, while he describes infants as seeing others' behaviors as like their own,[15] he seems to preclude infants from perceiving the world that these behaviors intend and from adopting this world at the same time that they adopt adults' behavior.[16] By referring to the neonates' behaviors as "imitative," I think we overlook what is actually most significant about these behaviors, namely, their collaborative character. Rather than simply perceiving adults, infants perceive *through* them; their focus is not adults' bodies as such but the meaningful world that is enacted by these bodies and that they, too, can participate in.[17]

In contrast to this research on neonates, research on slightly older infants does recognize that infants recognize other people as perceptive. Beginning when they are six to twelve months old, infants will follow an adult's gaze to an object and then join with the adult in interacting with this object; this phenomenon is generally referred to as "joint attention."[18] If the adult were, for the infants, merely experienced as perceived, then it would make no sense to speak of infants following the other's attention. While the infant could observe another's eye movements, she could never recognize these movements as attentive to the world.

Yet, as Beata Stawarska has argued, joint attention again is usually interpreted within the theoretical framework referred to as the "Theory of Mind" approach to social cognition.[19] That is, research on joint attention tends to begin with the premise that one can only perceive another's face as perceived. One's interaction with the other's face as perceiving, therefore, reflects one's development of a theory of mind that allows one to associate the other's face with perceiving. In other words, the theory-of-mind approach to social cognition argues for a form of the reasoning by analogy that Merleau-Ponty rejects. While research on joint attention acknowledges that we can interact with others as perceptive, this research, like research on neonate imitation, usually fails to recognize that we can directly perceive others as perceptive.

Consequently, research on joint attention again tends to misunderstand the collaborative character of the infant's behavior. By conceiving of joint attention as requiring a theory of mind, each person's separate perception of an object is understood as preceding their simultaneous interaction with this object; it is, in other words, because each sees the same object that they can then begin interacting with it together. In the situation described by Merleau-Ponty, however, the playful interaction between Merleau-Ponty and the baby was not grounded in each one's separate perception of the baby's fingers; rather, it was their mutual perception of the baby's fingers as being playfully bitten that enabled their playful interaction. In other words, it was perception itself, and not just the object, that was shared. Indeed, what Merleau-Ponty and the baby perceive before they begin interacting is quite different than what either perceives after they begin interacting; in their interaction, they perceive a shared landscape of possibilities, a landscape that neither perceived alone.

Additional evidence for an infant and caregiver's shared perception of the world is in fact found in research on the phenomenon referred to as "mutual gaze," and, in particular, by the work of psychologist

Daniel Stern.[20] In the phenomenon of mutual gaze, an infant and an adult, rather than looking together at something in the world (as in "joint attention"), look at each other's faces. As Stern notes, while it is uncommon for two adults to look into each other's faces for longer than a few seconds, an infant and a caregiver can look into each other's faces for thirty seconds or more.[21] Stern focuses on how, in instances of mutual gaze, the adult's facial expressions and vocalizations are not discrete events but, instead, form a specific tempo: "The regularity of tempo came as a surprise, perhaps in part because a mother can and does alter the degree of stress, or vigor, or amplitude of movements and sounds from moment to moment, thus giving the impression of changing tempo without actually doing so."[22] Moreover, he notes that an adult can regulate an infant's affect or arousal by modifying the tempo of her own activity:[23]

> "[W]hen an infant becomes overexcited and begins to emit the 'ah ah ah' sound of the fuss-cry, the caregiver will often speed up her rate of behavior to 'top' or override the baby's. She then slowly and progressively decreases the tempo of her speech or movement and in doing so acts like a pacemaker to quiet or soothe the baby."[24]

If the caregiver's behavior were simply something that the infant perceived, then it is not clear why increasing the tempo of these actions would excite the infant and decreasing the tempo of these actions would calm her. That is, it is not clear why there should be a significant change in the infant's mood even as the basic content of her experience remained the same. To understand the infant's relation to the adult's behavior, then, let us first think about our relation to our own behavior.

As I argued previously, our behavior is our perception of a world. Recognizing this, we can also recognize that, by changing the tempo of our behavior, we can significantly change the structure, or mood, of our experience. Indeed, we saw from Russon's analysis that rhythm is one of the founding dimensions of the meaningfulness of our experience. Thus, for example, if I am driving along a residential street, driving only slightly faster can change my experience from one of calm unconcern to one of anxious worry; although to an outside observer this change in speed may be barely noticeable, for me this change affects all I experience. More deeply, a single evening in which I do not see a friend or a single weekend in which I do not receive a call from my daughter may throw me into an emotional panic if I am habituated to a rhythm of daily socializing and weekly checking in with my children. At its very root, then, the tempo—the rhythm—of a behavior is integral to *how* it is perceptive, *how* it is a having of a world.

If we recognize, then, that the perception of the caregiver's behavior can inform *the way that* the infant perceives rather than simply being *something that* she perceives, we can recognize that the tempo of the caregiver's actions quite simply *is* the infant's experience of mood and that the caregiver, by changing the tempo of her actions, can also change the infant's mood. The caregiver's ability, by changing the tempo of her own actions, to calm an infant who is overexcited or excite an infant who is calm, thus suggests that mutual gaze is a form of shared perception. In her interactions with her caregiver, the infant comes to perceive the world as her caregiver perceives it. Their interaction becomes collaborative such that each is not so much acting *on* the other as acting *with* the other.[25]

For these reasons, then, I think we should recognize that, as Husserl's and Merleau-Ponty's phenomenological analyses of "pairing" indicate, we should see infant behavior from the start as a matter of *participation* rather than *observation*. In situations of joint attention and mutual gaze, we witness parent and child co-enacting a shared world, and this, I argue, is also the structure of the phenomenon typically referred to as "neonate imitation": the newborn behavior that is typically referred to as "imitation" should, thus, be considered instead as incipient play. With this background in place, let us now consider in more detail the implications of empirical research on infant-caregiver relations.

Infant-Caregiver Play Periods as "Pairings"

As I noted above, that infants do perceive others as perceptive is well-documented in the research on infant perception. Infants will, for example, treat their caregivers' eye movements as a gaze and pay attention to the objects that their caregivers are looking at rather than on their eye movements: this is the phenomenon of "joint attention," which we considered above. Another such phenomenon is "social referencing," which Saul Feinman, for example, defines as "a process in which one person utilizes another person's interpretation of the situation to formulate her own interpretation."[26] It can be shown that infants will treat their caregivers' facial expressions as expressing the emotional significance of what their caregivers perceive and will moderate their behavior accordingly. Yet these behaviors of "joint attention" and "social referencing" are generally thought to emerge only when infants are around nine months old.[27] One might think, therefore, that very young infants do not perceive others as perceptive and that the pairing relation described by Husserl only exists for older infants. Therefore, although I will turn to the discussion of social referencing in the next section, I will first reflect on behaviors observed in much younger infants. Specifically, I will look at situations of play.

Another reason that I do not want to begin by focusing on social referencing is that when we think about pairing relations, we might—as research on social referencing tends to do—focus on the perception of objects that surround those engaged in a pairing. Yet if we focus on infants' and caregivers' perceptions of the objects that surround them, we risk overlooking a possible "object" of perception in a pairing relation: the infants themselves. When interacting with very young infants, caregivers are often focused only on the infants themselves rather than on something beyond the infants. These dyadic infant-caregiver relationships—what Colwyn Trevarthen calls "primary intersubjectivity"—like the triadic infant-caregiver-object relations on which existing research on social referencing tends to focus—what Trevarthan calls "secondary intersubjectivity"—can take, I will argue, the form of a "pairing."[28]

In her book, *How Infants Know Minds*, Reddy notes that research on the experience of other people, including research on infants' experience of other people, has tended to think about our relation to other people from a third-person perspective. For example, researchers generally observe an interaction between two people and do not themselves participate in this interaction. Moreover, researchers may attribute this same third-person perspective to those whom they study; insofar as researchers themselves observe other people, they then conceive of others as doing the same. Reddy argues, however, that this third-person perspective tends to neglect some of our most potent experiences of others: experiences in which we are the "object" of others' attention:

> Imagine how you might feel when someone you love catches sight of you unexpectedly and smiles at you. The breath-catchingness and warmth in *receiving* that smile are likely to be rather different from *observing* that smile directed at someone else. . . . It matters powerfully whether the "other

mind" that you observe is turned towards you in engagement with you or towards someone else.[29]

Reddy argues, therefore, that we ought to take a second-person approach to research on the experience of other people; that is, we ought to focus on experiences of being directly engaged with another person—experiences of the other as a "you"—rather than on experiences of simply observing another person—experiences of the other as a "he" or "she."[30] Moreover, she argues that when we take a second-person approach to research on infants, we discover that there is no "problem of other minds" for infants: even very young infants experience others as aware of the infants themselves.

In arguing that even very young infants experience others as aware of them, Reddy draws on research on neonate imitation and infants' reactions to still faces.[31] Rather than reviewing this research, I will focus on some research that she does not focus on: research on infant-caregiver "play periods" by Daniel Stern, to whom I made reference in the previous section. Furthermore, rather than following Reddy's approach to infants' relations to others as a matter of knowing others' minds, I will approach these relations as a matter of perceiving others as perceptive. I will argue that Stern's account of infant-caregiver "play periods" offers support for the idea that the relation between young infants and their caregivers can take the form of a "pairing."

Stern refers to play periods as "purely social" because they involve only the infant and the caregiver. Following Stern, I focus only on "purely social" interactions between infants and their caregivers, but the conclusions I draw in this section might equally apply to what might be called "impurely social" interactions: routine practical activities like feeding, changing a diaper, and bathing. Indeed, Stern's emphasis on the purely social may reflect a commitment to Trevarthen's distinction between primary and secondary intersubjectivity in infant-caregiver communication, and this distinction itself may need to be rethought. That is, if the dyadic infant-caregiver relations that are most prevalent for infants younger than nine months take the form of a "pairing" and infants do not merely perceive their caregivers but perceive their caregivers as perceiving the infants themselves, then we will need to understand these dyadic relationships as forms of "social referencing," where it is the infant herself (or the caregiver herself) who serves as the "object" in an infant-caregiver-object triad whose significance is modulated for the infant by her perception of her caregiver's perception of it. Moreover, while acknowledging that triadic relations between infant, caregiver, and another object become increasingly prevalent in infants older than nine months, we may also need to acknowledge that such triadic relationships are not entirely absent prior to nine months.[32]

In his book *The First Relationship*, Stern draws attention to the frequency and character of "play periods" between young infants and their caregivers. Stern defines these play periods as:

> a bounded period of time, anywhere from seconds to many minutes, when one or both members focus their attention on the *social* behaviors of the other partner and react to these behaviors with *social* behaviors of their own. During the first half year of life, these play interactions are different than later forms of play, in that they are accomplished without recourse to any toys or artifacts or game rules. The interplay is with interpersonal moves.[33]

One of the specific play periods Stern describes involves a three-and-a-half-month-old infant, and he argues that infants become capable of the behaviors displayed in the play periods between about six weeks and three months of age.[34]

Play periods, Stern writes, often begin with the caregiver looking at the infant and forming a "mock-surprise expression."[35] The caregiver's "eyes open very wide, the eyebrows go up, the mouth opens wide, and the head is raised and tilted up slightly."[36] If the infant continues to look at the caregiver, the caregiver will then, while continuing to look at the infant, begin a series of vocalizations and/or nonverbal behaviors. This series is often repetitive, and it has a regular tempo.[37] The caregiver's behavior, Stern writes, takes the form of a theme and variations.[38]

While Stern generally focuses on caregivers' behavior during these play periods, he does discuss infants' behavior as well, noting that once caregivers initiate a play period, infants will often participate in this play period with vocalizations and/or nonverbal behaviors of their own. What I think deserves notice is how well the infants' behavior coordinates with that of their caregivers'. That is, out of all the behaviors that are possible for the infants, their behavior during these play periods is often quite similar to their caregivers'; for example, Stern found that the most common vocalizing pattern during play was the mother and infant vocalizing in unison. Moreover, if the behaviors of infants and their caregivers are not similar, they are often complementary.[39] For example, Stern describes a caregiver, during a break in breastfeeding, leaning closer to her infant,

> frowning, but with a twinkle in her eyes and her mouth pursed in a circle always on the edge of breaking into a smile. She said, "This time I'm gonna get ya," simultaneously poising her hand over the baby's belly ready to begin a finger-tickle march up the baby's belly and into the hilarious recesses of his neck and armpits. As she hovered and spoke, he smiled and squirmed but always stayed in eye contact with her. Even the actual tickle-march did not break their mutual gaze.[40]

Stern refers to the interaction just described as "taking the form of a repeating game," and he refers to several other interactions he discusses elsewhere in the book as games as well.[41] He refers to yet other interactions he discusses elsewhere as a "dance" or as like a dance.[42] Finally, in his discussion of the infant's behavioral repertoire, he refers to "jointly performed behaviors,"[43] and in his discussion of the structure and timing of infant-caregiver interactions, he refers to infants and caregivers as sharing a behavioral program or "[f]ollowing a shared program."[44] Although Stern does not discuss his own use of these terms, I think it is significant that he uses them in reference to the combined behavior of infant and caregiver and not to the behavior of one or the other. That is, it seems that these terms are meant to capture the quite remarkable coordination between the behaviors of the infants and those of their caregivers; these terms suggest that in these play periods, infant and caregiver are acting together—are playing *a* game or dancing *a* dance—rather than acting separately with each one playing his or her own game or dancing his or her own dance.

Stern's description has at least two important implications. First, this description, at least tacitly, already understands the behaviors of both infant and caregiver as perceptive, as expressive of, rather than independent from, consciousness. If the behaviors of infants and caregivers were considered solely as the movements of things within the world, that is, if they were considered only as objects that are perceived rather than as subjects who themselves perceive, then we could not describe the two as dancing together. We could only describe the two as making movements that might appear, to an outside observer, to be performed together but that must, in themselves, be understood as occurring separately. Dancing together—dancing *a* dance—requires each to be perceiving the other.[45]

Second, the description of infants and their caregivers as playing a game or dancing a dance implies that the infants not only perceive their caregivers but perceive their caregivers as perceptive. In other words, it implies that their relation is a "pairing." If the infants only perceived their caregivers, then the infants' perception of the world would remain distinct from their caregivers; the infants could thus play and dance, but they could never play or dance *with* their caregivers. Yet, if this were the case, one would expect that the caregivers' experience would be very different than the one described by Stern. Trying to dance with another person who remains oblivious to one's attempts to dance is quite frustrating, while trying to dance with another person who acknowledges one's attempts and reciprocates is quite enjoyable. To describe infants and their caregivers as playing *a* game or dancing *a* dance is thus to recognize, at least tacitly, that infants perceive their caregivers' vocalizations and movements as giving their specific situation a specific perceptual sense. The description implies that infants perceive their caregivers as perceiving the world as the "workshop" for a game or dance in which they, too, can participate.

While I have focused on infant-caregiver play periods, I think that understanding infants' relation to their caregivers as a "pairing" also helps make sense of Stern's observation about the effectiveness of caregiver behavior in regulating infant affect.[46] If infants only perceived their caregivers and did not perceive with them, it is not clear, particularly when infants become overexcited, why their caregivers' behavior can calm infants rather than just exciting them further. By understanding their relationship as a pairing, however, we can understand infants' affect as reflecting not simply their perception of their caregivers but the specific perceptual sense of the situation they are engaged in *with* their caregivers. If infants become overexcited, for example, a change in their caregivers' behavior can actually give their situation a calmer perceptual sense, thereby allowing the infants to become calmer. The child does not just "hear a sound" when the parent vocalizes and does not just "see the shape" of the parent's facial expression, but he grasps these "objective" phenomena *as* a way of perceiving the situation, and it is precisely *that perceived sense* of the situation that the child responds to.

Rather than thinking of very young infants as first encountering others as perceived and only later encountering them as perceptive, the work of Stern and others suggests that we can understand very young infants as first encountering others as perceptive. Furthermore, in contrast to the man famously described by Jean-Paul Sartre in *Being and Nothingness* who is frozen with shame when another sees him peering through a keyhole, young infants seem to experience others' perception of them as enabling rather than as petrifying.[47] Thus, even if triadic instances of social referencing only become prevalent when infants are nine months or older, we need not conclude that younger infants simply do not experience others as perceptive. Instead, we should recognize that infants begin by experiencing others as perceptive of the infants themselves and then later come to experience others as perceptive of additional objects beyond them. Indeed, the work of Stern and others suggests that infants' primary experience of others consists of a "pairing" relation, and it is the absence of a perceptual "pairing" that is the secondary experience that must gradually develop within the child's experience. If this is the case, then infants do not need to discover that others perceive them; rather, infants need to discover that—in certain situations—others do *not* perceive them. Likewise, infants will first experience their feelings and emotions as perceptible to others and only later discover that they are often not; that is, infants will first experience all "objects" of their experience as public and only later, once they begin to notice what caregivers do not perceive about them, come to experience some of these "objects" as private.

Caregiver "Availability" and the Impact of Pairing Relations on Infant Perception

So far, I have argued that the relation between very young infants and their caregivers takes the form of "pairing." Now, I will focus on some of the implications of this pairing relation for older infants by turning to some research on social referencing and considering the impact that infants' pairing relations might have on their developing perception of the world.

In a study conducted by Suzanne Carr and colleagues, pairs of eighteen-to-thirty-month-old infants and their mothers were put in a room that had some toys tethered in one corner.[48] They found that the infants whose mothers sat facing the toys spent most of their time playing with the toys. Infants whose mothers had their backs to the toys or were behind a partition, however, often left the toys, which were not within the mother's visual field, and moved to a place that was within the mother's visual field.

If infants' relation to their caregivers consisted simply of seeing that they were present, then one would expect that both the infants whose mothers had their backs to the toys and the infants whose mothers were facing the toys would play with the toys. That the infants whose mothers had their backs to the toys tended to leave the toys to move closer to their mothers suggests that these infants were not satisfied with simply seeing that their mothers were present and were looking toward them for something more. Carr and colleagues interpret the infants' behavior as evidence that infants' usual relation to their caregivers consists, not of seeing that they are present, but of seeing their faces: "Although the children in our experiment were willing to tolerate some loss in visual [face-to-face] contact, they were clearly disturbed by this and, in fact, left the toys much of the time to reestablish this contact."[49]

I think that this interpretation does not sufficiently grasp the significance of the description by Carr and colleagues of the infants who could not see their mothers' faces as moving within their mothers' visual field. This description suggests the infants' behavior is not just a matter of keeping their mothers' faces within their view but also a matter of keeping themselves within their mothers' view. That is, this study suggests that infants' usual relation to their caregivers involves experiencing their caregivers as perceptive.

That infants' usual relations to their caregivers involve perceiving them as perceptive is attested to by a study conducted by James Sorce and Robert Emde. Sorce and Emde placed pairs of fifteen-month-old infants and their mothers at one end of a room, a stranger at the other end, and a toy area in the middle. Half of the mothers in the infant-mother pairs read a newspaper for fifteen minutes; these mothers' faces were clearly visible to the infant, but their attention was "fully engaged in reading."[50] The other half of the mothers did not read but, instead, "were instructed to monitor their infants' activities and to respond empathically and appropriately throughout the entire sequence while remaining seated."[51]

Sorce and Emde found that infants whose mothers read a newspaper explored less and exhibited less pleasure than those infants whose mothers looked at them. Although those infants whose mothers read did play with the toys in the room, their play "was characterized by a serious, businesslike involvement,"[52] and they were "clearly vigilant of their [mothers'] behavior."[53] They also stayed further away from the stranger in the room and were more likely to leave the area where the toys were located and move closer to their mothers, where they then "waited patiently."[54]

Sorce and Emde interpret these behaviors as evidence that infants usually relate to their caregivers' "emotional availability" rather than their faces. They define "emotional availability" as a caregiver's communication "through her ongoing behavior that she is aware of the infant's presence, is monitoring ongoing activity, and is available to respond empathically and appropriately."[55] As they write, "especially in unfamiliar surroundings, when the consequences of engaging in exploration cannot be clearly predicted, infants intermittently need to 'check back' with their mothers, looking at her face and ongoing behaviors in order to confirm her availability."[56] I now want to consider the implications of this interpretation.

Given that the faces of both groups of mothers were visible, there is little difference between the two groups when the mothers are considered solely as perceived objects. When the mothers are considered as perceived perceivers, however, there is a dramatic difference between the two groups: the perception of one group of mothers was occupied with their newspapers, while the perception of the other group of mothers was occupied with their infants and their toys. That the infants whose mothers were in the former group behaved differently than the infants whose mothers were in the latter suggests, then, that the infants did not simply perceive their caregivers but also perceived with them. In other words, it is implied in Sorce and Emde's attribution of the difference in the infants' behavior to a difference in their mothers' "availability" that infants' relations to their caregivers take the form of a "pairing."

Furthermore, not only were the infants not indifferent to what their mothers perceived, but they were also not merely curious. That those infants whose mothers read a newspaper often withdrew from the toys and waited while those infants whose mothers looked at them often continued exploring the toys suggests that infants cease, in a certain sense, to perceive what cannot be perceived with their caregivers. That is, while infants do not become literally blind to whatever is imperceptible to their caregivers, they cease to perceive these things as inviting their involvement (a point investigated in more detail below). In other words, implied in Sorce and Emde's attribution of the difference in the infants' behavior to their mothers' "availability" is that infants' "pairing" relations to their caregivers are not occasional events but, instead, are the condition for their perception of the world as a "workshop" for their projects.

Understanding the relation of infants and their caregivers as a pairing not only helps make sense of the infants' behavior in this second study, but it also helps make sense of the observation by Carr and colleagues that when infants' mothers sat behind a partition, these infants often "substituted talking for looking and proximity; that is, increased talking compensated for decreased visual and proximal contact."[57] In other words, it seems that when infants cannot establish a visual pairing with their mothers, they seek to establish this relation with language.[58]

One final study, conducted by Sorce and colleagues, not only provides further evidence that infants' relations to their caregivers can take the form of a pairing but also offers some insight into the unique significance of this pairing.[59] The study involved a visual cliff, a steep drop-off covered by plexiglass that can be crawled across safely by an infant. Twelve-month-old infants were placed on the shallow end of the visual cliff, while their mothers were placed on the deep end of the cliff. When the infants approached the drop-off, most infants hesitated and looked toward their mothers. The mothers were instructed to show a facial expression of either happiness, fear, interest, anger, or sadness. All of the infants whose mothers expressed fear, and almost all of the infants whose mothers expressed anger paused at the edge of the cliff and then retreated from it. Almost all of the infants whose mothers showed expressions of happiness or interest crossed over to the deep side of the cliff. Infants whose mothers showed an expression of sadness waited by the edge of the cliff and continued to look toward their mothers.

If the infants simply perceived their caregivers as objects, one would not expect the caregivers' facial expressions to have any effect on the infants' behavior. After all, why would an object next to the visual cliff have any bearing on the perception of the visual cliff itself? That the infants' behavior reflected their caregivers' facial expressions suggests it was the cliff *as perceived by* their caregivers (or, more exactly, their perception of the children's relationship to the cliff), and not simply the conjunction of the cliff and their caregivers, that the infants perceived. In other words, the infants' behavior in this study suggests that the infants' relations to their caregivers were a matter of "pairing"; the infants saw their caregivers' facial expressions as making sense of the visual cliff as either a route to be followed or an obstacle to be avoided, and it was the visual cliff, as it was first perceived by the caregivers, with which the infants then interacted.

Beyond offering further confirmation that the relationship of an infant to a caregiver should be understood as a pairing, this experiment also helps reveal a particularly critical aspect of this pairing. The world need not be perceived identically by every caregiver; for example, in the experiment just discussed, some caregivers, by expressing happiness, perceived the visual cliff as passable, while others, by expressing fear, exhibited it as impassable. Moreover, each of these ways of perceiving the world is not equally valid; the visual cliff is, in fact, passable. However, infants are not in a position to judge whether their caregivers' perception of the world is valid since the world as perceived by their caregivers is the world that they perceive. While infants whose caregivers perceive some single thing as impassable when it is, in fact, passable, will not likely be much affected by this, infants whose caregivers consistently perceive things that are passable as impassable could come to perceive the world, in general, as an obstacle. How, then, the particular caregiver with which a particular infant is paired perceives the world will be of lasting significance for an infant's perception of the world, a point we will investigate more fully when we discuss Russon's work below.

Pairing and Trust

I have argued that all of these empirical studies support the phenomenological idea that the child's experience of her caregiver is primarily a matter of "pairing"; that is, the child perceives her caregiver *as* an "other." The caregiver is not perceived simply as an object, but neither is her subjectivity a "problem"; instead, the child perceives the caregiver *as another perceiver* by collaborating with her perceptually. I want to make a further point about the essential *affective* dimension of this pairing, and to do this I will return to Stern's studies of mutual gaze.

Stern's understanding of mutual gaze finds support in Hanne De Jaegher and Ezequiel Di Paolo's work on participatory sense-making. De Jaegher and Di Paolo define participatory sense-making as "the coordination of intentional activity in interaction, whereby individual sense-making processes are affected and new domains of social sense-making can be generated that were not available to each individual on her own."[60] De Jaegher and Di Paolo cite a case of mutual gaze described by Stern as an example of a particular kind of participatory sense-making in which "through coordination of sense-making, one of the interactors is oriented toward a novel domain of significance that was part of the sense-making activity of the other."[61] In this case, a mother repeats the phrase "I'm gonna getcha," each time lengthening both the time it takes her to say the phrase and the time she pauses between the phrases. In doing so,

Stern writes, "the caregiver progressively 'stretches' the interval of the anticipated beat and in doing so increases the degree of discrepancy from the expected and the infant's excitement."[62] Likewise, De Jaegher and Di Paolo argue that the affect regulation described by Stern is possible because "the infant is oriented towards a change of affective state through his participation in coordination with the mother's tempo."[63]

Yet even as Stern and De Jaegher and Di Paolo's discussions of mutual gaze reveal its essentially collaborative character, I think they overlook its emotional significance. Stern often describes the infant and her caregiver as equal partners in their interaction; he writes, for example, that "both partners can regulate the amount of effective stimulation impinging on the infant"[64] and that "both mother and infant can readjust their behavior to bring the level temporarily back into an optimal range."[65] Likewise, De Jaegher and Di Paolo define social interaction as "the regulated coupling between at least two autonomous agents,"[66] and they do not modify this definition when discussing interactions between a caregiver and infant.

I think, however, that while infants have a kind of autonomy, their autonomy is very different than that of adults. Infants can act spontaneously, and their activity can have an impact on their interactions with their caregivers; in this sense, infants are autonomous. Yet unlike adults, infants have little or no prior experience of either their own behavior or the behavior of others. They cannot, therefore, evaluate the meaning their behavior enacts in light of past interactions with other people. For example, an infant whose caregiver maintains the tempo of their interaction even when the infant becomes overwhelmed and begins to fuss cannot know that, with another person, her fussing would succeed in slowing the tempo of their interaction. Thus, rather than being able, as an adult might, to attribute the failure to slow the tempo of their interaction to her caregiver rather than herself, an infant can only experience her actions as ineffective, and thus may, even when she is with another person, give no indication when she is becoming overwhelmed. She cannot, in other words, experience an inattentive caregiver as inattentive if she has never experienced an attentive caregiver. In addition, even if infants are, in some way, dissatisfied with their caregivers' behavior, they have little, if any, means to address this. Infants, unlike adults, cannot simply break off their relationships with their caregivers and begin a relationship with someone else.[67] The landscape of shared possibilities infants create with their caregivers, therefore, is not one landscape among others within a larger world; this landscape simply is their world.

Thus however active infants are in these collaborations with their caregivers—and they can be quite active—the role infants play in these relationships is that of an *initiate*; they must participate, and yet they, unlike adults, must participate with little if any ability to understand the impact that these collaborations will have on their life. Infants thus depend on their caregivers to initiate them into a shared world that is both worthwhile and fulfilling, a world that prepares them for interactions with people other than their caregivers. That is, they depend on their caregivers to initiate them into a shared world that is truly shared, a world that others besides their caregivers will perceive.[68]

The pairing of child and caregiver is, in other words, a matter of *trust*. In entering into their caregivers' perception of the world, infants "live" their caregivers as reliable guides to this world. Infants' trust in their caregivers is their perception of the world they share with their caregivers as real; their trust is their perception of their shared world as a route toward, rather than an obstacle to, future collaboration with others. In devoting themselves to the world as they perceive it with their caregivers—in continuing to practice, for example, the specific ways of handling people and things that they began practicing with their caregivers—infants enact their trust in their caregivers. It is this theme that has been the focus of much of Russon's phenomenological research on childhood development.

Russon on Pairing as the Institution of Personality

In the previous section, I argued that the infant's role in her relationships with others was that of an initiate. In participating with others in their way of having a world, she had to trust that this way of having a world would support, rather than impede, her further development. To develop the existential implications of this point, I will turn to Russon's discussion of the significance of childhood experience in *Human Experience* and in two papers, "Between Two Intimacies" and "The Virtues of Agency."

As adults, Russon writes, we live in "an important and essential way . . . as self-defined individuals, independently negotiating with an independent reality."[69] Yet, he argues, this experience of "independent, self-reliant individuality" develops from an "experience of familial intimacy in which we, as children, live from a non-reflective and bodily sense of a sharedness of identity with another."[70] The child's experience begins as the experience of a family member rather than a unique individual. The family is a structure of cooperative self-definition: as a family member, "[o]ne does not regard oneself as the one and only significance, but as one significance among many: . . . the truth is not 'me' but 'our thing.' "[71] The child's initial experience, then, is that of a participant in his family's world (an idea discussed in chapter 2 in relation to Russon's analysis of "eating disorders"); his initial experience is of "we" rather than of "I." The possibilities the child experiences the world and others as affording are initially the possibilities of his family: "It is our family—our group of familiars—that first defines for us where we fit into intersubjective relations and, consequently, what will count as the values by which 'we' must approach the world, and by which we must contact reality. Our family defines for us our proper place, and, indeed, the place of propriety—of value—itself."[72]

Our adult experience of a clear distinction between ourselves, other people, and the world is, therefore, not an innate given. Indeed, childhood can be defined *phenomenologically*, as "a form of experiencing that is characterized by different forms of subject-object relationships than those which define adult experience";[73] for children, there "is not an interpersonal connection *in contrast to* an engagement with things; on the contrary, definitive of childhood experience is the fact that it is a process *simultaneously* of growing into the world, growing into a shared experience with someone else (a primary care-giver), and growing into a sense of self."[74] For example, Russon writes, as a child plays with a toy truck in the company of her mother, the possibilities the toy truck holds for the child are inextricable from her mother's responses to her behavior:

> The child pushes the toy truck over the floor, for example, but as she does so she looks up, expectant, into her mother's face: for the child, the practice of using her body and moving the toy is intertwined with the search for the mother's approbation. Though from our outside perspective, mother and toy are radically different realities, with the perspective of the child, they are not thus differentiated: a phenomenological description of the child's experience as it is lived must acknowledge that dealing with the toy is an aspect of dealing with "Mama."[75]

As I argued above in the discussion of Sorce and Emde's research, the "pairing" of child and parent is not one occasional event among many;

it is, rather, the condition of the infant's perception of the world in general.

Just as the objects with which we interact can be resistant or receptive to our desires, so, too, can the other people with whom we interact. Russon's point is that these two sources of resistance or receptivity are not strictly differentiated for the young child. For the young girl playing with the truck, for example, her mother's resistance to her running the truck into the cat is inextricable from the possibilities she experiences the truck as affording her. Like the child's experience of the cliff as passable or impassable in the experiments of Sorce and others, those interactions with the truck to which her mother is receptive are experienced by the child as tenable, while those interactions that meet with her mother's disapproval are experienced as less tenable or even untenable: "What counts as success, then, in the child's navigation of the inherently interpersonal fabric of its experience of self-others-world, is substantially defined by the attitude—the will—of the significant other(s)."[76] Indeed, those interactions that meet with her mother's disapproval may cease to be experienced as possibilities at all. What the child experiences things as affording her is defined by her relations with others in concert with her physical capabilities rather than by her physical capabilities alone; the child's reality is simultaneously intersubjective and worldly. Indeed, her relations with others may obscure or conceal possibilities of which she is physically capable or reveal possibilities that expand her physical capacities beyond those she presently possesses (an issue that Simone de Beauvoir addresses explicitly in her discussion of childhood in *The Second Sex*).[77] For the child, the reality of the world is inextricable from the reality of her familial others. The child's experience of her interactions with the world as tenable requires the "validation and endorsement" not just of the world but also of her family.[78]

Moreover, Russon argues, the child's experience of the world and of others is also inextricable from the experience of her own self. In *The Divided Self*, the phenomenological "anti-psychiatrist" R. D. Laing argued that a child is not born with a secure sense of "self"; a child must develop a sense of her own validity, a sense of herself as mattering to both the world and others.[79] Developing this sense, however, requires the validation of the world and of others, and this is the focus of Russon's analysis. The relations between a child, her caregivers, and the world offer the child:

a kind of self-interpretation. This is not a theoretical self-interpretation, in the form of someone saying the sentence that "you are an agent in the world who can function well and take things on"; but an emotional self-interpretation, a bodily self-interpretation, a practical self-interpretation, communicated to the child through touch, through bodily interaction, and so on.[80]

The child's experience of her interactions with the world and others as "tenable" is equally an experience of her own validity: "[V]ariations in the status of the mother-world reality directly influence the child's self-experience. The motherly disapproval of pushing the truck into the cat, for example, directly produces a feeling of unhappy unworthiness in the child. . . . The truck-reality is inseparably "made of" plastic, mother's mood and the child's sense of self-worth."[81] It is, Russon argues, only insofar as the world and others are generally receptive, rather than indifferent, to the child that a child develops a secure sense of self.

Russon emphasizes that this secure sense of self is a critical component of the child's sense of herself as an *agent*, as someone who acts upon, and is not simply acted upon by, the world and others: "The early development of the child is the gradual process of transformation from experience as something simply undergone—the 'happening' of a texture of emergent feelings, motions, sounds, etc.—to experience as something substantially shaped by doing."[82] A critical task of others' relationships with a child is to develop the child's ability to be, and to experience herself as, an agent, as someone "who can 'own' a change in the world . . . and can express her or himself in and as such a change in the world."[83] Russon describes this developing sense of agency as characterized by "virtues," by the secure actualization of various potentialities of our being-in-the-world: the virtues of "primary self-confidence," "primary courage," and "primary creativity." He calls these virtues "primary" because they are the "very fabric of a self" rather than being "a self-conscious view of a subject about itself"[84]: they are the terms in which we *live* our sense of self. Primary self-confidence is "the basic sense that I am real and that I matter"[85]; primary courage "is the further ability to take that self into the realm of another that does not give confidence"[86]; primary creativity is a "lived recognition of oneself as a generative source."[87] All of these fundamental ways of *being* a "self" are themselves, Russon argues, rooted in and reflective of (formative) intersubjective relationships.

The child's experience of behaving in ways that her familial world welcomes is simultaneously her experience of herself as worthy of this welcome. Her sense of herself as an agent, as someone who can effect change with respect to both the world and others, is dependent on her family's receptivity to at least some of the possibilities to which the world is receptive. If the child is ever to experience herself as *independent of* her family—which we expect of mature individuals—she must first be allowed by her family to *participate in* their shared world. The child's development of a sense of herself as an independent source of meaning and value requires the collaboration of others.

Of course, not every family provides the validation necessary for a child to develop an adequate sense of herself as an agent. Without such an adequate sense, the child will never fully develop out of her experience as a child and a family member and into the life of an individual: "Without a secure sense of world as a place where it is proper for one to act, without a secure sense of oneself as someone who can go forth and do something creative and transformative, without a secure sense of the world as a place where one shares life with other people, one is fundamentally crippled in one's ability to be a functioning independent adult."[88] The most severe of these problems are the sort studied by Laing—the psychoses. Yet even for those children whose families enable them to develop a sense of themselves as agents, the transition to adulthood may not be entirely unproblematic. These less severe problems are the neuroses that Russon studies in *Human Experience*, to which I drew attention at the end of chapter 2.

One of the main points that Russon stresses is the necessarily specific and contingent form of any individual's family life: the shared world the child participates in with her family is always *particular*.

> We do not begin, as it were, fully connected to reality, but have a particular opening, a particular clearing within which we can develop and expand. . . . The same is true of our initial participation in the reality of intersubjective life. We do not begin as full participants in a fully formed "we," but have, rather, a particular and determinate contact with others that is the arena within which we can establish routes for grasping, posturing ourselves in, and tasting human reality as such.[89]

Moreover, the particularity of our family's way of having a world will not initially be experienced as particular: "[P]ractices are not appropriated *as* idiosyncratic or optional, but as the essential fabric of its engagement with the world."[90] Consequently, we, as children, grow up in and into a contingent way of interpreting ourselves and our world, but the contingency of this interpretation is not itself apparent to us.

A family, insofar as it is only one family among many families, does not exclusively determine what is proper for the world, for others, and for ourselves. Although we, as children, live our family's way of having a world as an unquestionable absolute, our family's way of having a world is not, in fact, a universal truth. Thus, the sense of ourselves as agents that we have developed as children may be profoundly shaken when we begin to interact with a world and with others who are not familiar. Our familiar ways of engaging with the world and with others may not be welcomed by the world and the others who exist beyond our family. Others' sense of what is proper will differ from our family's, and we will need to learn how to negotiate these new senses of propriety if we are to maintain our sense of ourselves as agents.[91] For most of us, negotiating such a change is possible. This, however, is not a given, but rests on our having already developed an adequate sense of independent agency. If it is our very sense of agency that is compromised by the history of our formative intersubjective life, however, making the transition to such independent adulthood may be an impossible task for us.

Conclusion

Russon's phenomenological analyses of family life and childhood development, then, demonstrate the incredible stakes that are involved in the pairing relation that Husserl and Merleau-Ponty argue to be the essential structure of human intersubjectivity and that psychological research shows to be formative of parent-caregiver relations. Other people are not just one of the many things in the world that we might experience. On the contrary, other people are our very route into experiencing for ourselves—indeed, into experiencing ourselves *as* "selves." *How* I am able to be "I" is something that is only accomplished through my habitual embrace of the (ideally, enabling) perception of my subjectivity by others.

An important aspect of our continuing development, then, will be to recognize the particularity of the structure of experience we developed as children and to be open to its transformation. Habitual structures of experience that were enabling in the context of family life may be quite disabling in the context of life beyond the family, and they will need to be transformed if we are to flourish as adults. We will carry on, now, to look more directly at the kinds of relationships with others that we develop as independent adults; specifically, we will look at the distinctive meaning of *sexuality* as an experience of another person.

4

Recognition and Sexuality

Introduction

Over the course of a day, many of us encounter a large number of people, and our relations to most, if not all, of these people are quite impersonal. That is, rather than relating to them individually, as irreplaceable in our experience by any others, we relate to each of these people generically, as replaceable in our experience by others. My relation to a person at my workplace, for example, is usually defined primarily by our positions within the company that employs us both, and my relation to this person will be largely identical to my relation with any other person who holds the same position. Likewise, my relation to a person I pass on the street is likely defined primarily by our status within the political institutions that govern us both, and my relation to this person will be largely identical to my relation to any other person who holds the same status. Moreover, we are often quite content for such relations to be impersonal. That is, we are often quite content to have the question of how we will interact with our co-workers answered by company policy and the question of how we will interact with people we pass on the street answered by local, state, and federal law. Indeed, if we all had to negotiate personally how we make contact with all these people, our jobs would probably not exist, and it would probably be impossible to take a leisurely walk outside.[1]

Yet even as our adult lives are filled with quite impersonal relations, they are also filled with more personal relations. Our relations with friends and family members, as well as our relations with, for example, a therapist or the imam at our mosque, are usually defined far more uniquely than our relations with, for example, co-workers or people we simply pass on the street; that is, these relations are usually far more reflective of the richly developed rhythm and harmony of our experience that distinguish one person's experience from that of any other person. Furthermore, these relations are generally far more meaningful for our experience of ourselves and the world. My basic sense of my own self-worth, for example, is usually far more at stake in my relation with a close friend than it is with a random person on the street. In other words, these adult relations, more so than other adult relations, are pairings whose existential significance is on par with, although certainly not identical to, the childhood pairing relations I discussed in the previous chapter. Within the domain of our personal relations, I will focus on sexual experience as offering particularly powerful examples of pairing relations between adults.

In this chapter, I will take up sexuality as the second avenue, after the experiences of childhood, into grasping the ways that intersubjectivity is at play in our experience *below* and *behind* the level of theoretical cognition. As was the case in our study of childhood "pairing," in our study of sexuality we are similarly investigating an experience in which we perceive the other *as* perceptive: specifically, we shall see, in sexuality we desire the other's desire. Furthermore, in our sexuality we typically explicitly acknowledge to ourselves that how we figure in the eyes of another matters to us. Yet, even though we may be cognitively aware of our desire to be desired, sexuality is not, for that reason, a "theoretical" or "mental" experience of the other; on the contrary, sexual intersubjectivity is bodily, affective, intuitive, and so on. In this chapter, we will precisely investigate the parameters of sexuality as an *intentionality*, in Husserl's sense: a *bodily* intentionality that intends the other *as* other, and, indeed, *as* a body.

I will turn to part 1, chapter 5 of Merleau-Ponty's *Phenomenology of Perception*, "The Body as Sexed Being," for the core, phenomenological understanding of sexual intentionality. I will then consider how the rich implications of the central insight of this chapter are more fully worked out in studies of sexuality by Beauvoir, in *The Second Sex*, and by Russon, primarily in *Bearing Witness to Epiphany*. We will see that, rather than turning inward and approaching sexual desire as a kind of mental event, we ought, instead, to turn outward and see sexual desire as an engagement with *another* and within our *bodies*. Further, I will argue that while both Beauvoir and Russon criticize norms that typically pervade sexual experience, they nonetheless understand sexual experience as having a normative dimension. I will distinguish, as Beauvoir does, between erotic experience that is or is not "authentic," or as Russon does, between erotic experience that is or is not a "betrayal" to further develop the sense of the implicit normativity of experience that we have already witnessed through our study of trust in childhood experience.

First, I focus on Merleau-Ponty's conception of sexual desire as an embodied intentionality that grasps other bodies as subjects. Then, by drawing on the theme of "recognition" (*Anerkennung*) from G. W. F. Hegel's *Phenomenology of Spirit*, I explore the specific form of recognition that is enacted by our bodies as attracted and attractive to other bodies: in sexual desire, I argue, what our bodies reach for in other bodies is for these other bodies to reach for our own reaching of their bodies; that is, in being drawn toward other bodies, our bodies are not so much putting other bodies within our reach but, instead, putting our own bodies—precisely as subjects rather than objects—within the reach of others. In this context, I discuss our unique vulnerability in sexual desire. What we will see, especially through our discussions of Beauvoir and Russon, is the way that fundamental matters of value—of ethics—are inseparable from our sexual intentionality. Before turning to Merleau-Ponty's chapter, though, I will first return to the themes of family life with which we ended our last chapter and draw on Russon again to clarify how sexual experience is situated within the broader context of our development.

Childhood Intimacy and Adult Intimacy

As I argued in the previous chapter, childhood experience primarily entails joining one's family in the shared world established by the other family members long before one was ever born. As Russon writes, "as newly emerged children, we do not generate our social customs from ourselves and we do not see other options, but rather find ourselves in a situation that already operates according to customs—that operates according to particular, already determinate customs."[2] Children have their place within the shared world of their family largely defined for them, and although a child can, certainly, contribute to her family's development of new practices, for the most part, children fit into a world of already created meanings rather than creating meanings of their own.

Yet, while childhood experience is largely an experience of submitting oneself to a world established by others, healthy development entails having this initial submission enable a sense of independent individuality. Describing childhood intimacy, Russon writes in "Between Two Intimacies" that it "is not just a good in itself but, further, has work to do in our human development in that it is the essential context for supporting the development of those dimensions of selfhood that allow one to function as an independent adult operating in the objective world."[3]

While it is profoundly disabling never to be allowed to participate in the "we" that is family life, it is also profoundly disabling never to be allowed to grow out of this "we" and into an "I." If she is to be healthy, the child's development into her family's practices must allow her further development into a self-reliant individual with unique practices of her own. In other words, a person must move beyond the unchosen "pairings" of childhood, in which the "otherness" of intimate others has yet to be appreciated, to chosen "pairings" of adulthood, in which the "otherness" of intimate others is a key concern.

In contrast to childhood experience, then, adult experience entails recognizing that one's family's practices are not the only tenable practices for engaging with the world and with others; it entails recognizing that, beyond maintaining our already established practices, we can revise these established practices and also create new practices. Although we will always likely retain many of the practices that defined family life, our very capacity to live apart from our families gives us the opportunity to live the world differently than our family does. Furthermore, adult experience entails encountering others who are not familiar and do not live the world as our family does. In this chapter, I will focus on sexual experience as a particularly potent form of such encounters. While childhood experience is largely a matter of joining the already established shared world of one's familiars, adult experience, I will argue, is largely a matter of establishing shared worlds with those who are precisely not familiar. As Russon writes in *Human Experience*, "we must come to find our family members, whom we initially take to be naturally given as special and necessary (proper), to be strange and contingent, and we must develop *for ourselves* new familiarities with strangers, who we come to recognize as legitimately (properly) making demands upon our identities."[4] In sexual experience, this reckoning with those who are not familiar, this reckoning with those who live the world in ways that are very different from our own, takes place in bodily intimacy. Let us now reflect on this "bodily intimacy."

Sexuality as a Bodily Intentionality

To grasp the sense of the unique domain of sexuality, it is helpful initially to take note of the placement of Merleau-Ponty's chapter within the *Phenomenology of Perception* as a whole—namely, between chapter 3, "The Spatiality of One's Own Body and Motricity," which examines how our body as moving and grasping gives our world a practical significance, and chapter 6, "The Body as Expression and Speech," which examines how our body as speaking gives our world a social significance.[5] As this positioning of Merleau-Ponty's chapter suggests, his study of sexuality is a description of a dimension of our experience that is neither exactly practical nor exactly social, a dimension that involves other people but that involves them primarily in bodily interaction rather than in speech or politics. Sexuality is a quite unique form of our experience of others.

How, then, do others appear to us in sexual desire? In our everyday experience, we can be drawn to other people's words and ideas, but we can also be drawn to other people's bodies. We are, we say, "attracted" to these other bodies, and we approach and come into contact with these bodies in ways that are quite different from the ways that we approach and come into contact with other things and bodies. But how should we understand this attraction? First, Merleau-Ponty argues, our body is not attracted to other bodies in the way that one magnet is attracted to another. Our attraction, unlike that of the magnets, is a form of *experience*; as Merleau-Ponty announces in the title for the first section of this chapter, "Sexuality is not a mixture of 'representations' and reflexes, but an intentionality."[6] Thus, Merleau-Ponty approaches sexual desire as Husserl approaches perception or imagination: as a particular way in which things appear to us. Just as the table that we perceive appears to us differently than the table that we imagine, the body we desire sexually appears to us differently than the body we do not.

Yet, while sexual desire is intentional, this intentionality, Merleau-Ponty argues, is, like the motor intentionality we considered in our initial discussion of phenomenology, a matter of the body rather than of the self-reflective consciousness. That sexual desire is a bodily intentionality has at least two implications.

First, we must recognize that the way that our bodies approach and make contact with other bodies in sexual situations generally *is* our experience of these other bodies as sexually desirable rather than being a *sign* of our experience of these other bodies as sexually desirable. We do not need to think that other bodies are sexually desirable and then make an explicit decision to begin bringing our bodies into contact with them before our bodies begin to do so; our bodies do this of their own accord. As Merleau-Ponty writes, "erotic perception is not a cogitation that intends a cogitatum; through one body it aims at another body, and it is accomplished in the world, not within consciousness. . . .

[D]esire comprehends blindly by linking one body to another."[7] This does not imply that sexual relations are not—or should not be—matters of careful reflection or that we are, in some sense, not responsible for the ways that we interact with others sexually. Rather, it draws attention to what such careful reflection presupposes: our inextricability from a realm in which our bodies' engagements with things and others can always enact our experience of certain others as sexually desirable or undesirable and can always be experienced by others as our being drawn toward or away from them in ways that they find desirable or undesirable. I may, for example, find that my eyes have been drawn to a particular person sitting by me and have been gazing at her. Of course, this other person may have found my eyes' gaze upon her quite undesirable, although she could equally experience my eyes' gaze upon someone other than her also as quite undesirable.

Second, we must recognize that the bodily intentionality of sexual desire is an experience of other bodies as themselves intentional. In sexual experience, our bodies are not attracted to other bodies simply as objects; rather, our bodies are attracted to others as subjects. To claim that our bodies are attracted to other bodies simply as objects would be to ignore that our sexual experience is permeated by concerns—like that of being modest—that only appear in our experience of other subjects.[8] Yet what, precisely, is the nature of the subjectivity that our bodies are attracted to in other bodies? Here, I think, Merleau-Ponty's discussion of Kurt Goldstein's and Adhemar Gelb's brain-damaged patient, Schneider, is helpful.

Johann Schneider was a young soldier, injured in 1915 by an exploding mine. Shrapnel entered his brain, and this resulted in many dramatic perceptual and behavioral problems for him. In other chapters of the *Phenomenology of Perception*, Merleau-Ponty investigates the visual, conceptual, linguistic, and motor problems Schneider faced. Generally, Schneider was impaired in his ability to grasp wholes and in his ability to engage effectively with abstract or novel situations. Schneider also developed problems sexually.[9]

Schneider, Merleau-Ponty writes, is not attracted to particular female bodies; for him, "it is the personality that makes a woman attractive, for, when it comes to their bodies, they are all the same."[10] Moreover, when Schneider touches a woman, the experience "only produces a 'vague feeling' or the 'knowledge of something indeterminate,' which is never enough 'to launch' sexual behavior or to create a situation calling for a definite mode of resolution."[11]

Schneider's sexual experience stands out as different from our experience in general because we normally experience embodiment as an integral—rather than a merely optional—feature of subjectivity in general and of sexual subjectivity in particular.[12] As the phenomenological description of our experience shows, unlike Schneider, we do not experience other bodies as merely being associated with other subjects; that is, we do not experience others' subjectivity as existing solely in the form of "minds." Rather, in experience generally, as we have seen, and quite expressly in sexual desire, we experience others' subjectivity as embodied; we experience others' bodies as, in Merleau-Ponty's words, "animated by a consciousness."[13] Thus, our sexual attraction to other bodies does not typically occur only after we have ascertained—through conversation with these bodies or through close observation of their behavior—that these other bodies contain minds. Rather, our bodies are often immediately attracted to other bodies as subjects. Indeed, as Russon writes in *Bearing Witness to Epiphany*, "Erotic experience is the fundamental bodily recognition of the presence of another person as a person. Erotic attraction is the stirring of the other in me, in my body."[14]

As bodies, we are things in the world, the objects of the perception of others, but we are also subjects, and to recognize what one is encountering *as* a subject is more than the simple recognition of it as an immediately present object. Implicit in sexuality, then, is the need to carry out, at a bodily level, the recognition of another subject as a subject.[15] What it takes to recognize a subject adequately, to recognize a subject *as* a subject, is the theme of Hegel's study of the dialectical relationship of recognition in his *Phenomenology of Spirit*, and a short digression on this work is quite crucial to understanding the phenomenological description of sexuality in Merleau-Ponty and in the parallel works by Beauvoir and Russon.

Hegel on Recognizing Subjects as Subjects

The most basic way I have of apprehending myself, Hegel argues in the *Phenomenology of Spirit*, is as desire.[16] In the experience of desire, I relate to myself, in practice rather than as an explicit assertion, as determining reality; in desire, the terms in which my object exists are the terms in which it exists *for me*. Hegel writes,

> [S]elf-consciousness is *desire* in general . . . [and] has a double object: one is the immediate object, that of sense-certainty and perception, which however *for self-consciousness* has the character of a *negative*; and the second, namely, *itself*, which is the true *essence*, and is present in the first instance only as opposed to the first object. . . . Certain of the nothingness of this other, it explicitly affirms that this nothingness is *for it* the truth of the other; it destroys the independent object and thereby gives itself the certainty of itself.[17]

In this experience of desire, I grasp a critical dimension of my existence as a subject: as a subject, I am irreducible to any thing that I experience. Nonetheless, I am only a subject insofar as I experience something. Any thing that exists exists for me, and yet, qua desiring subject, I only exist insofar as there is something for me:

> Self-consciousness which is simply *for itself* and directly characterizes its object as a negative element, or is primarily *desire*, will . . . learn through experience that the object is independent. . . . Desire and the self-certainty obtained in its gratification are conditioned by the object, for self-certainty comes from superseding this other: in order that this supersession can take place, there must be this other.[18]

Thus, while I might first understand the things that I experience as completely inessential to me, my own experience demonstrates that this is not the case and demands that I develop a more adequate understanding of myself.

The inadequacy of my understanding of myself as desire becomes particularly apparent, Hegel argues, in my experience of another subject. Another subject is not only a being whom I experience; she is also a being by whom I am experienced. Describing this situation, Hegel writes, "Self-consciousness is faced by another self-consciousness; it has come *out of itself*. . . . [I]t has lost itself, for it finds itself as an *other* being."[19] This experience of being experienced by another subject challenges my understanding of myself as determining reality. As experienced by another subject, I am determined rather than determining. My experience of another subject demonstrates, then, that I am not absolutely definitive of reality; everything that exists does not simply exist for me.

Yet even as my own experience demands that I revise my understanding of myself, I need not actually answer to this demand. In experiencing another subject, I may attempt to maintain my understanding of myself as absolutely definitive by trying to eliminate the other subject. Hegel describes this experience of the "life and death struggle" to show that, although I may indeed succeed in killing the other subject, my own experience testifies to the inadequacy of this way of relating to another subject.[20] In trying to kill the other subject, I relate to her as an object rather than a subject, and yet it was only as a subject that the other was a challenge to me. The struggle to the death does not, therefore, address what is fundamentally at issue in my experience of the other, namely, her existence as an experiencer by whom I am experienced. It is the other's experience of me that I must address in my relation with her.

Insofar as I have experienced another subject, my own experience demonstrates that I am not absolutely definitive of reality. I must contend with other subjects who also define reality. Furthermore, my own experience teaches me that relating to these other subjects as objects does not address the real issue I confront in my experience of them: that I am experienced by them and that I am, therefore, not absolutely self-defining.

Rather than try to eliminate the other subject, I might also pursue another strategy to evade the challenge presented by her subjectivity: I might seek to dominate her; that is, I might attempt to dictate the other's experience to her and thereby demonstrate that I am absolutely definitive. Hegel describes this relationship of "master and slave."[21] In pursuing the other's enslavement rather than her death, I seek the other's submission; that is, I do relate to the being whom I experience as a subject, and I try to have my domination established from within that other's own subjectivity. If the other subject does, in fact, acknowledge her subordination to me, that is, if we jointly relate to one another in a way that prioritizes my experience over hers, I may continue to understand myself as absolutely definitive. Yet, Hegel argues, once again, my own experience demonstrates the inadequacy of this self-understanding.

Two subjects can only relate to one another as master and slave if both experience their relation as one of master and slave. If either I or the other subject insists on struggling to the death, for example, no master-slave relation is possible. The master-slave relation, then, relies on a kind of agreement between the two subjects. Inasmuch as this relation not only requires me to recognize the other as my slave but also essentially requires the other to recognize me first as her master, my power to define the other's experience is not, therefore, within my power. I do not actually control what gives me control over the other, namely, the other's experience of me. I am only able to define the other's experience insofar as she first defines me as defining her experience. In the master-slave relation, then, I do not actually define absolutely what I take myself to be defining absolutely: the other subject's experience of me continues to determine "my own" experience.

Relations governed by recognition are determined mutually. Nonetheless, although all relations of recognition are implicitly mutual, this mutuality is generally not explicitly acknowledged. When I dominate another person, although I implicitly understand myself as desire for another's desire, I fail to understand the reciprocity of our relation. I alone do not constitute my own experience. My experience, my subjectivity, is never simply mine but is, instead, always mediated by other subjects' experiences of me. Thus, rather than seeking to avoid this mediation in my relations with others—which is impossible—I should, instead, explicitly acknowledge it. Hegel describes this situation of equal recognition: "Each sees the *other* do the same as it does; each does itself what it demands of the other, and therefore also does what it does only in so far as the other does the same. Action by one side only would be useless because what is to happen can only be brought about by both."[22] Rather than seeking to control others' experiences of me, I should acknowledge that their experiences of me are fundamentally beyond my control and that our experiences must be developed cooperatively.

In our phenomenological reflections, we have seen that we are bodies and subjects and that it is the distinctive challenge of sexuality to be the bodily recognition of a body *as* a subject. It is not surprising, then, that Merleau-Ponty asserts that the dialectic of recognition described by Hegel is thus at play in sexuality. He writes: "To say that I have a body is thus a way of saying that I can be seen as an object and that I seek to be seen as a subject, that another person can be my master or my slave, such that modesty and immodesty express the dialectic of the plurality of consciousnesses and that they in fact have a metaphysical signification. The same could be said of sexual desire."[23] Sexuality is a fundamental way that we experience that there are other subjects in the world and we desire these other subjects to recognize us as subjects. To explore these issues of recognition within sexuality, let us first turn to *The*

Second Sex, in which Beauvoir richly explores the complex development of the experience of subjectivity within sexuality.[24]

Sexuality as Embodied Recognition

None of us lives our body only as an object; all of us—and more fundamentally—live our bodies as subjects. Yet, Beauvoir argues, some of us—in general, as well as in sexual experience more specifically—live our bodies as realizing our subjectivity more fully than others. Our bodies are not all equally capable of moving within and contacting the world in ways that are supportive of our projects—erotic or otherwise. Insofar as erotic desire is a bodily intentionality, then, erotic experience will require, at the very least, that our bodies move and come into contact with other bodies in ways that support—rather than undermine—our erotic desire. Beauvoir describes typical differences between men's and women's lived bodies insofar as they are illuminative of the basic embodied dynamics of sexuality, and describing the typical development of male sexuality, she writes,

> For man, the passage from childhood sexuality to maturity is relatively simple: erotic pleasure is objectified; now, instead of being realized in his immanent presence, this erotic pleasure is intended for a transcendent being. The erection is the expression of this need; with penis, hands, mouth, with his whole body, the man reaches out for his partner, but he remains at the heart of this activity.[25]

Throughout the discussion that follows, I will draw on Beauvoir's views regarding differences between men's and women's lived bodies insofar as they are illuminative of the basic embodied dynamics of sexuality, without thereby assuming or implying that these differences necessarily map onto individuals who are coded as "male" or "female"; here, what is especially powerful is her observation that erotic experience requires a body that "remains at the heart" of its activity, a body that sustains its subjectivity in its interactions with others. I will refer to such a body as "expressive."[26]

Although we might take bodies' expressivity for granted, this capacity is, Beauvoir argues, habituated rather than innate. We do not begin life capable of moving within and contacting the world in ways that are supportive of our projects; we are not born—both literally and metaphorically—with the ability to "handle" the world. Indeed, our first movements are often more fumbling than skillful, and our contact with the world generally unfolds on the world's terms rather than our own. As infants, the world reaches us far more than we reach the world. Even as reached by the world, our bodies are indeed still subjects rather than mere passive objects; nonetheless, when our sensitivity to the world is not augmented by expressivity, our bodies realize subjectivity in only a very minimal sense. It is one thing to give meaning to the world in one's intention and imagination; it is another to give meaning to the world in the world itself. Our bodies realize subjectivity more fully as our movements and our contact with the world become skillful. Developing an expressive body, however, takes effort. Our bodies must practice moving in and making contact with the world skillfully in order to become expressive.

Yet while men's bodies have generally been habituated to expressivity, Beauvoir argues, women's have not.[27] Social norms encourage men's bodies to be active; social norms encourage women's bodies, on the other hand, to be passive. Not only are women discouraged from making the movements and contact that would develop their bodies as expressive, but they are actually encouraged to restrict their movements in and contact with the world. Women often, therefore, practice limiting their movements in and avoiding contact with the world, and thus the absence of habits of expression is exacerbated by the presence of habits of submission[28]; "There are beings whose life slips by in an infantile world because, having been kept in a state of servitude and ignorance, they have no means of breaking the ceiling which is stretched over their heads."[29] Women's bodies confront several other challenges specifically to their erotic desire that men do not. The greater externality and visibility of men's genitals in comparison to women's genitals, Beauvoir argues, makes it simpler for men to live these parts of their bodies, like the rest of their bodies, as expressive.[30] Furthermore, she notes, women's bodies, unlike men's, face the risk of unwanted pregnancy.[31]

Insofar as women's bodies, unlike men's bodies, have not been habituated to expression—insofar as, as she writes in *Ethics of Ambiguity*, they have not received an "apprenticeship of freedom"—women's bodies are unpracticed in the kinds of movement and contact that their erotic desire demands.[32] Thus, while women have often imagined reaching out for another person, they find themselves unprepared for the bodily reality of erotic experience. As Beauvoir writes, "During the engagement, dating, or courtship period, however basic it may have been, she continued to live in her familiar universe of ceremony and dreams . . . It was still possible to make believe. And suddenly there she is, gazed upon by real eyes, handled by real hands: it is the implacable reality of this gazing and grasping that terrifies her."[33]

Beauvoir notes that a body's expressivity is often enacted by its hands; we live the contact between our hands and the world, perhaps more than the contact between any other part of our body and the world, as our bodies' reaching the world rather than the world reaching our bodies. I will use the term "hand" as a synonym for an expressive body, but it is important to remember that other parts of the body, and, indeed, the body as a whole, can be lived as "hands" in this sense. While men tend to practice living their bodies as such "hands"—as expressive—women tend to practice living their bodies as what I, drawing again upon Beauvoir's language, will call "skin"—as submissive. Beauvoir writes, "Her sensuality is located both in her skin and in her hand, and their exigencies are in opposition to one another"[34]; women's bodies thus work against their erotic desire. Women have practiced limiting movement and avoiding contact, while their erotic desire demands that they move toward other bodies and make contact with them. Thus, although men's enactment of erotic desire is not, as we shall see shortly, entirely unproblematic, men's bodies at least do not immediately undermine their own erotic desire.

In light of these reflections, one might think that achieving an authentic erotic experience would simply require that women practice living their bodies as "hands" rather than as "skin." Yet while erotic desire can only be fulfilled by an expressive body, Beauvoir suggests that a body's expressivity alone is not sufficient to fulfill erotic desire. Even when men's expressive contact with other bodies results in orgasm, Beauvoir writes, "pleasure is not the only aim; it is often followed by disappointment: the need has disappeared rather than having been satisfied."[35] Likewise, Beauvoir writes, women often experience contact between their genitals and their partners' hands—even when this contact brings them to orgasm—as unsatisfying. These women's inability to live their bodies expressively may, certainly, contribute to their dissatisfaction, but Beauvoir attributes their dissatisfaction to another source: "Many shy away from being caressed by the hand because it is an instrument that does not participate in the pleasure it gives; it is activity and not flesh; and if sex itself does not come across as flesh penetrated with desire but as a cleverly used tool, woman will feel the same repulsion."[36] In these cases, Beauvoir suggests, the woman's erotic desire remains unfulfilled, not so much because she fails to live her body as expressive but, instead, because her partner fails to recognize her body as expressive and, instead, recognizes her body as submissive.[37] That is, rather than welcoming the contact that she initiates, her partner is indifferent—or even hostile—to it. Here we can see that our expressive, sexual contact, more than simply seeking the pleasurable experience of orgasm, actually seeks a form of mutual recognition.

What our bodies reach out for in erotic desire, Beauvoir argues, is quite different than what our bodies reach out for in other forms of bodily intentionality. Indeed, Beauvoir argues that the "object" of erotic desire is, ultimately, not an object at all. Erotic desire is not reducible to a desire for orgasm with another body, and erotic desire is not ultimately fulfilled through one body's skillful management of its contact with other bodies. Rather, erotic desire intends other bodies as subjects. Our bodies reach out for other bodies as themselves reaching out—as alive to our advances—and we live the contact between us as their recognition—or misrecognition—of our expressivity. Even as we live our bodies as expressive, others live their bodies as expressive, too, and the contact that enacts our expressivity may be at odds with the contact that enacts others' expressivity. It is thus that we see something closely akin to the dialectic of recognition described by Hegel acted out within our sexual lives.

Even as our bodies seek contact that other bodies will welcome, others may challenge or pull away from, rather than embrace, our contact with them. Faced with the fear of possible rejection, for example, one might find another's sexual expressivity threatening, and one might live one's body's expressivity as a suppression of others' expressivity. Analogously, fear of being threatening or fear of living with the responsibility of shaping interpersonal life may lead us to be submissive in our own sexuality, inviting the domination of another.

Yet, Beauvoir argues, we profoundly misunderstand erotic desire if we think erotic desire intends other bodies as participants in relationships of domination and subordination. In relation to the example discussed earlier, women's dissatisfaction with their partners does not, Beauvoir suggests, result from women's inability to dominate men; women do not want men's bodies to cease being "hands" and to become, instead, "skin." Instead, women want men's bodies to cease being hands that dominate and become, instead, hands that are, as she says in the lines I quoted, "flesh." "Woman," she writes, "would be spared many difficulties were man not to trail behind him so many complexes making him consider the love act a battle: then it would be possible for her not to consider the bed as an arena."[38] In other words, the problem is not that men are insufficiently submissive to women's expressivity but that men live women's expressivity as necessarily opposed to their own.

The demands of one's body as "flesh," in contrast to the demands of one's body as "skin," are not necessarily contrary to the demands of one's body as "hand." Indeed, in living their bodies as "flesh," men—any persons who live their sexual bodies expressively—will not be rendered *incapable* of fulfilling their erotic desires; instead, they will be rendered capable of fulfilling their erotic desires truly for the first time.

Insofar as recognition is at issue in sexual desire, then, our bodies seek far more than mere physical contact with other bodies. In sexual desire, our bodies seek validation of our *subjectivity*, but of our subjectivity precisely *as embodied*.[39] Our bodies bring us within others' reach so that these others can reach us precisely as reaching for them. In other words, in sexual desire, our bodies seek to be attractive to other bodies in their very attraction to these other bodies. That is, our bodies seek to be attractive to other bodies not as objects that merely conform to other bodies' desires but as subjects with desires of our own.

When we are thinking about movement and contact between bodies, we often focus, I think, on examples in which our bodies initiate this movement and contact. My hand makes contact with another person's hand, for example, when my hand moves away from the table and on top of the other person's hand. Yet other bodies can also, of course, initiate the movement that results in contact between our bodies. My hand makes contact with another person's hand, for example, when she moves her hand away from the table and lays it on top of mine. In both cases, however, all of the bodies involved exist as subjects, and thus, in both cases, every revelation of others' bodies to us is simultaneously—and unavoidably—the revelation of our bodies to them. Moreover, this is a revelation of our bodies, not just as objects, but also as subjects. In the contact between embodied subjects, we feel others' bodies as embracing or recoiling from this contact. Thus, in the contact between embodied subjects, no body is absolutely active, and no body is absolutely receptive. As Merleau-Ponty writes, "sexual experience is like a passive experience, given to everyone and always available, of the human condition in its most general moments of autonomy and dependence."[40]

In other words, sexual situations may be defined by a kind of reversibility of touching and touched.⁴¹ Moreover, we might think of this reversibility as integral to the fulfillment of sexual desire. Insofar as sexual desire is a desire for recognition, our bodies cannot reach what they are reaching for in other bodies unilaterally.⁴² While our bodies can force other bodies to make contact with our bodies, our bodies cannot force other bodies to be attracted to our bodies' attraction to them. Our bodies can only reach what they are reaching for, then, if other bodies experience our bodies reaching as precisely what they are themselves reaching for. Our bodies' intentionality must fulfill other bodies' intentionality if it is to fulfill its own. We must, in other words, recognize the strange character of sexual experience. If our sexual desires are to be fulfilled, these desires must ultimately be pursued in concert with—rather than in opposition to—the desires of others. We are, in sexual situations, dependent on others. Yet this dependence, while it can certainly impinge on our autonomy, is also the only route to the fullest realization of our autonomy. Sexual situations are situations in which our autonomy is most fully realized only to the extent that the others' autonomy is also most fully realized.

Of course, we can, as we have just seen, bring our bodies within reach of other bodies only to have these bodies reach for us as objects rather than subjects or reach for us as subjects simply to dominate us. As Merleau-Ponty claims in "Man Seen from the Outside," most of our relationships with others take the form of master and slave, and in "The Body as Sexed Being," as we saw, he notes that our sexual relations are no exception.⁴³ Nonetheless, sexual situations, if they are ultimately to fulfill our sexual desires, must be situations in which our bodies' autonomy is not achieved at the price of other bodies' autonomy.⁴⁴ In sexual situations, bodies can reach for one another as reaching, and, indeed, they must reach for one another as reaching if their recognition of one another is to be adequate. As embodied subjects who are both touching and touched by other embodied subjects, we are subjects whose subjectivity is ultimately realized through—and not in opposition to—our dependence on other subjects.

Sexuality and Interpersonal Vulnerability

In his discussion of Schneider, Merleau-Ponty writes that Schneider "has ceased posing to his surroundings that silent and permanent question that defines normal sexuality."⁴⁵ We must recognize that this question is first articulated not in words but in our bodies' perception of other bodies. Yet recognizing the question as silent does not preclude us from putting it into words; it simply precludes us from forgetting that these words have their source in bodies that enact their own form of communication. What our discussion so far indicates is that this question might be articulated as: "Will other bodies be attracted to my body's attraction?"

Our study of recognition in sexuality has explored the implications of the fact that this is a question that our bodies can never answer for themselves and must, instead, turn to other bodies to answer. Our bodies cannot, on their own, guarantee that our attraction to other bodies will be reciprocated with others' attraction to our bodies. Sexual situations are, therefore, situations of great vulnerability, and thus, like childhood intimacy, sexual intimacy is ultimately a matter of trust. Because it is such matters of intersubjectivity that are at stake in our sexuality, we can be injured sexually by inadequate recognition just as much as we can be injured by physical abuse. In *The Second Sex*, Beauvoir investigated how our adoption of the fundamental roles of masculine and feminine sexuality reflects unequal approaches to our founding experiences of "autonomy and dependence," as Merleau-Ponty puts it. In *Bearing Witness to Epiphany*, Russon investigates parallel themes as they are alive in—"embodied" in—our sexual practices. Thus, while what is at stake in sexual experience is mutual attraction and the mutual realization of our autonomy, the vulnerability entailed by sexual experience often leads us to deny these stakes, and Russon investigates the ways in which our sexual practices can embody such denials and thus amount to betrayals of trust—of the intersubjective bonds that are constitutive of our experience.

Our behavioral betrayal of our intersubjective bonds, Russon argues, can take two basic forms. First, we can betray our bonds with others—themselves inherently shared experiences—by acting as if a bond belongs to just one of the people between whom the bond exists: "Betrayal is pretending that what is 'ours' is simply 'mine' or 'yours.' Betrayal, that is, can take the form of theft—claiming what is ours to be solely mine—or refusal—claiming what is ours to be solely yours."[46] Second, we can betray our bonds with others by acting as if how these bonds are to be enacted has already been determined independently of us: "This second form of betrayal is the attitude that pretends that a bond does not require judgment and appropriation, that it is not ambiguous and shared but is an obvious, settled piece of reality."[47] Let us look further at these ways in which our sexuality is thus simultaneously an enactment of, and an honest or dishonest commentary on, our intersubjectivity.

We often live our sexual relations with others by attempting to eliminate the vulnerability of our embodied subjectivity to another embodied subjectivity. We treat sexual relations as situations that involve only one embodied subject rather than two, and thus commit the first forms of betrayal described by Russon: theft and refusal. As he writes in "Why Sexuality Matters,"

> Ideally, we should thus experience a situation of two people happily enjoying their shared experience of mutual desire. But because that other person has the power to give or withhold his or her desire for us, we can also feel captive to that desire and thus treat the other person's desire as a "prize" to be won or a challenge to be overpowered. We may thus live out our sexual life as a practice of seduction, trying to turn ourselves into a desirable object that captivates the other. . . . [Or,] in order to minimize the threat to our own self-esteem that might come from opening ourselves to the other and failing to satisfy them or, worse, being rejected by them, we can become cold with our partners, closing off our emotional attachment so as to avoid the situations that could be sites of possible pain. Or, again, we may become possessive or controlling, trying to use force to contain the constant threat that that other person's desire might turn elsewhere.[48]

On the one hand, we may attempt to have our bodies unilaterally achieve what can only be achieved reciprocally, such that our sexual experience devolves into one of domination where our bodies evade their existence as touched and continue to press toward other bodies even as these other bodies rebuff our advances. On the other hand, we may attempt to have other bodies unilaterally achieve what can only be achieved reciprocally, such that our sexual experience devolves into one of subservience where our bodies evade their existence as touching and fail to recognize that even a lack of movement toward or away from other bodies is, nonetheless, still a way of touching these bodies. In each of these different scenarios, one partner is living in fundamental denial of the shared character of the relationship, either trying unilaterally to control it ("theft") or pretending not to be implicated in it ("refusal").

We also treat sexual relations as situations governed by preexisting standards and thus commit the second form of betrayal described by

Russon. Both our bodies and other bodies may retreat into explicit codes of sexual conduct or implicit sexual norms and act as if these codes or norms—rather than the unique desire of uniquely embodied subjects—determine how sexual experience should unfold. In *Human Experience*, Russon describes how this second form of betrayal can take the form of a "normal" sexual life that might otherwise seem, in relationship to the first form of betrayal, to be quite equal and open. Let us see how that is so.

Our culture not only provides us with numerous images of sexual life, but it also provides us with a framework within which to interpret these images as better and worse realizations of sexual life. Relations with beautiful people—where the terms of "beauty" are themselves strongly specified culturally—are portrayed as definitive of sexual life, genital intercourse is portrayed as definitive of sexual fulfillment, and intercourse in which both partners reach orgasm, for example, is portrayed as superior to relations in which both partners do not. This model of "normal" sexuality can seem to us to be obvious and natural; yet, Russon argues, if we take our culture's definition of a fulfilling sexual relationship as definitive for our own sexual relations, we actually deny the reality of our sexual relations. Sexuality, Russon writes, "is the sphere in which our initiative, our freedom, is decisive."[49] Sexuality is precisely the sphere in which we must determine for ourselves what we want from each other: "It is *up to us*: this is the core of erotic experience. In erotic life, we feel the reality of sharing, of original, creative co-action."[50] If, then, we act as if what is decisive in sexual relations is not our own initiative but, instead, the norms of our culture, we betray our bonds with others; to pursue sex as a "a site for posturing, for conforming to the rule of an image: 'this is what we're supposed to do' . . . is antithetical to the inherent character of sexuality as the arena of cocreation, that is, the arena where we are beyond alien rules."[51] Erotic life, in contrast to family life, does not demand our adherence to what has already been established; erotic life demands our openness and creativity.[52] Insofar, then, as we experience a "normal" sexual life as compelling, our sexual life is, in the sense previously mentioned in chapter 2, "neurotic." What defines a sexual situation as neurotic is not that we experience ourselves as compelled to engage with others sexually, but that we experience ourselves as compelled to engage with others sexually in conformity with social norms: "The neuroses are the ways in which a multiply figured situation of contact is at odds with itself, such that its inherent trajectory toward freedom is inhibited by its habitual realization of potentiality."[53] If we adopt—as most of us surely have—our culturally defined images of sexuality as models for our own behavior, we have in fact set ourselves at odds with ourselves and have adopted rules for managing our sexuality that run counter to its basic trajectory toward the mutual autonomy of ourselves and our partners.

In treating the fundamental indeterminacy of sexual experience as determinate, that is, in trying to answer unilaterally and definitively that "silent and permanent question" that can only ever be answered in a way that is both collaborative and open-ended, we ultimately thwart our own sexual desires. Similarly, in attempting to eliminate our vulnerability, in attempting to prevent any diminishment of our embodied subjectivity's autonomy, we also prevent the fullest realization of this autonomy. What our sexuality actually calls for, on the contrary, is precisely vulnerability—vulnerability to the other and vulnerability to the indeterminacy, the question, of sexual desire itself. It is in actually being open to this call that we can, as Merleau-Ponty writes at the end of "Man Seen from the Outside," "prepare the ground for those rare and precious moments at which human beings come to recognize, to find, one another."[54]

Sexuality and Freedom

"Nothing," Beauvoir writes, "is murkier than *contact*."[55] Contact is murky because our contact with the world is simultaneously the world's contact with us. As embodied subjects, we do not stand apart from the world we experience. This ambiguity of agency and passivity is heightened in our contact with other people, because others reach for—or away from—us as we reach for them: our very touching of them depends on their allowing themselves to be touched. Erotic desire is the pursuit of a contact that is the welcoming of our reach by that of the other.

Russon's critique of a "normal" sexual life and Beauvoir's identification of "authentic erotic experience" reveal that erotic experience has a normative dimension, but the norm they identify, unlike the norm of "normal" sexual life, precisely concerns the extent to which mutual creativity, rather than any specific behavior, is present or absent in erotic experience. As Russon writes, "Sexuality is by its nature resistant to 'normalization' and rules, because of their static, impersonal, and imposed nature, but this does not mean that sex is without norms; its norms, however, are the immanent norms that develop through the contact between the partners, the norms of human contact itself with all that they entail."[56] What erotic desire ultimately intends is for others to "reach out" for us as expressively as we "reach out" for them. As a desire for mutually expressive contact, erotic desire will never be fulfilled through the suppression of others' expressivity. Others can only truly welcome our expressivity by being expressive themselves. Indeed, in an authentic erotic experience, we delight in each other's expressivity. As Beauvoir writes, "the lovers can experience shared pleasure in their own way; each partner feels pleasure as being his own while at the same time having its source in the other. The words 'receive' and 'give' exchange meanings."[57] Our bodies reach for other bodies' expressivity as in collaboration—rather than competition—with our own expressivity: "[T]he dimension of the other remains; but the fact is that alterity no longer has a hostile character."[58] In an authentic erotic experience our contact with other bodies is as expressive of these other bodies as it is of our own bodies. For this reason, the kind of contact that will create a genuine erotic reality cannot be determined ahead of time[59]; as Russon argued, those involved cannot turn to familiar social norms or even to their own previous experiences to determine what kind of contact to pursue. Those involved can only turn to one another and work out, in their contact with another, what kind of contact will be mutually expressive; "What is necessary for such harmony are not technical refinements but rather, on the basis of an immediate erotic attraction, a reciprocal generosity of body and soul."[60] Any identification of specific behaviors as unconducive to an authentic erotic experience will thus reflect the absence of a mutually creative context for these behaviors rather than a criticism of the detached behaviors in and of themselves.

"Authentic" erotic experience encompasses, therefore, a much wider variety of sexual behaviors than those included in "normal" sexual life. Indeed, "authentic" erotic experience may often include behaviors that deviate from the behaviors identified with a "normal" sexual life: "not . . . wait[ing] for the proper time and the proper person, or . . . being interested in 'wrong' practices."[61] Moreover, since what defines erotic experience as "authentic" is mutual creativity, we cannot simply repeat behaviors we have witnessed others practicing, behaviors we have practiced in our own past relationships, or even behaviors that we practiced in the past within our present relationship. It is the mutually creative context of the specific behaviors that have realized others' or our own past authentic erotic experiences, rather than the specific behaviors themselves, that we ought to emulate if our present experience is to be authentic. Thus, while authentic erotic experience does not require our present behaviors to be completely different from past behaviors, it does require that we recognize our present behavior as not determined by any past behaviors. Seeking to have present behavior conform to past behavior precludes experience from being authentic, even if similarities between present behavior and past behavior do not. Indeed, authentic erotic experience, by definition, must encompass behaviors that have yet to be created and practiced. It is a norm of approaching other people's behaviors as well as our own past behaviors as reminders of our freedom, as encouragements to, rather than constraints upon, our own creativity.

Erotic desire, then, is the revelation of those involved as irreducible to any already given determination, and this is simply another way of saying that it is the revelation of those involved as *free*. Erotic desire is thus a domain that implies that the full realization of our freedom requires the full realization of others' freedom: in our dependence on the other's freedom, our freedom is ultimately enhanced. Achieving a genuine erotic reality requires that our bodies attest to the reciprocity of human freedom in their contact with other bodies. In a genuine erotic reality, our bodies live the truth of Beauvoir's declaration in the *Ethics of Ambiguity*: "To will oneself free is also to will others free."[62]

Conclusion

With both our discussion of childhood intersubjectivity and our discussion of sexual intersubjectivity, we have been led to see that our intersubjectivity is not just a "neutral" fact about our existence. On the contrary, intersubjectivity is a reality that we shape through our enactment of it: who *I* am depends upon who *we* are, and *who* we are depends on *how* we are. Furthermore, this enactment, precisely because it is a matter of whether and how a subject is recognizing a subject—a freedom is recognizing a freedom—has a fundamentally normative character. In the case of childhood development, it is the child's basic formation as a person that is at issue, and in our sexual experiences, it is our recognition as free, expressive agents that is at stake; in both cases, our intersubjective relations are fundamentally matters of vulnerability and trust. The epistemological and metaphysical issue of "the problem of other minds"—of whether and how we recognize other subjects as subjects—is thus unavoidably an ethical issue.

Conclusion

The Concrete Ethics of Lived Experience

We began by asking, "What do we perceive?" and we noted that, typically, we imagine that what we perceive is a simple, physical object. Our initial discussion of phenomenology led us to see, however, that this falls far short of an adequate description of the form of our perceptual life. Our subsequent, detailed study of our experience of other people has led us to see that the other person, in particular, is typically not perceived as a simple physical object in the manner that we typically suppose. First, the other person is a subject, and not just an object, and therefore the other is *ap*perceived. As Husserl says: in perceiving the other I am perceiving something that cannot itself be present as such—I perceive the ("absent") other *through* what is actually present. Second, though, my most important experiences of others do not have those others as thematic objects. Instead, other people—the important other people in my life—are typically part of the *form* of my experience: I perceive other things *through* them. Third, other people are not indifferent things that can easily be "held apart" from one's own identity: whether at the formative level of childhood development, or at the adult level of the formation of erotic relationships, others affect us intimately; both from the point of view of healthy development and from the point of view of existential fulfillment, we are *already* involved with others, and how we care for and are cared for by others is highly consequential. This last point, then, indicates, finally, the inherently ethical character of our relationship with others. I conclude this book, therefore, with a reflection on how this phenomenological study of the experience of other people opens up distinctive avenues for ethics.

Although ethics has always been a prominent theme in the phenomenological tradition, it is surely the work of Emmanuel Levinas that has most prominently thematized the distinctive character of ethical experience and its intrinsic relationship to the experience of others. Levinas refers to this experience of another person as such as the experience of the "face." In the experience of the face, I experience someone whose way of being-in-the-world is irreducible to my way of being-in-the-world. The face cannot be assimilated into my world. It is not, as Levinas writes in *Totality and Infinity*, "finite." Instead, the face is "infinite": it is "The presence of a being not entering into, but overflowing, the sphere of the same."[1] The experience of the face is of a reality that is fundamentally unfamiliar—a reality that precisely announces to me the nonultimacy of the terms of my perspective: "The Other remains infinitely transcendent, infinitely foreign."[2] To encounter another person *as such*, Levinas argues, is to feel an imperative not to reduce the other to the terms of my world.

This imperative is an—is *the*—ethical imperative: "This infinity, stronger than murder, already resists us in his face, is his face, is the primordial expression, in the first word: 'you shall not commit murder.'"[3] In the experience of the face, I experience that I ought not to treat this person as if she were a mere thing that I experience. In this sense, the epiphany of the face is a kind of challenge, inasmuch as it announces a reality that outstrips my "I can," for, although I can use my worldly powers against the body of the other—the other as an occurring thing in the world—I cannot affect the reality of the Other as such. Thus, Levinas writes, "[t]he expression the face introduces into the world does not defy the feebleness of my powers, but my ability for power."[4] Of course, I can commit murder; that is, I can, having experienced another person as an independent source of meaning and value, act as if I did not experience her as such; I can treat her as a mere thing. Yet I can never experience this mode of relating to her as adequate. I experience myself *as murdering* her rather than as simply using her as I might use any other thing. Thus, even if I try to deny the experience of the face, I merely confirm the experience of the face: "The epiphany of the face is ethical. The struggle this face can threaten *presupposes* the transcendence of expression."[5]

Yet, Levinas argues, although the experience of the face is in a sense a challenge to me, I need not experience the face as hostile: "This presentation is preeminently nonviolence, for instead of offending my freedom it calls it to responsibility and founds it."[6] The opening that the other offers me to the domain of ethical responsibility is not an inhibition of my freedom, but is, on the contrary, my invitation—my initiation—into the fulfillment of my experience of freedom. Indeed, as we saw Beauvoir write, "To will oneself free is also to will others free."[7] Thus, while the experience of the other is inherently a challenge to the self-defined domain of my experience and thus a "threat" to my individual identity—the authority of my "I"—the relation to the other as such is actually supportive of my individuality: the other gives me the opportunity to live more fully as an intrinsically creative source of meaning, a source, that is, for *co*-creative responsiveness.

We began our phenomenological study of the experience of others by asking how one subject can perceive another *as* a subject. Levinas's remarks draw our attention to the fact that this apparently "epistemological" question is inherently an ethical imperative that defines our experience; as Russon similarly writes, "The epiphany of the other is the foundation of ethics."[8] What our phenomenological study allows us to see, therefore, is that, in working out the concrete specificities of how we "know" others, we are mapping the terrain of ethics. It is this point that is Russon's central thesis in *Bearing Witness to Epiphany*.

In the focal chapter of *Bearing Witness to Epiphany*, "Responsibility: On Ethics," Russon argues that our intimate bonds are the critical site for our lived negotiation of the ethical imperative that constitutes our experience of other people as other: "[H]ow we create and shape our bonds is one of our deepest ethical issues (an issue generally ignored in most discussions of ethics, which focus, typically, on what are taken to be the acts of isolated individuals or else on issues of social groups beyond the realm of the interpersonal)."[9] The specific form that a bond takes is ethically significant: a bond can answer more or less adequately to the ethical imperative of the other.

> With another, we make a bond. . . . The bond, like an act of expression, will be our way of behaviorally claiming ourselves, our way of saying who we are. Some bonds are more honest, some less, some more informative, some more concealing, some open to richer development, some more limiting. . . . Through our bonds with each other we can express the richness of our freedom, or we can unite in an effort to conceal our humanity. The character of the bond will be manifest in how we behave rather than in what we explicitly assert about ourselves.[10]

The ethical question that pervades the intimate bonds we form is whether we form these bonds in affirmation or in denial of the freedom and responsibility that is constitutive of intersubjective relationships; as Russon writes, "The real issue for assessing whether the relationship is healthy is . . . whether the trajectory of this self-contained unit—the self-defined bond of the couple—is open to or closed against self-transformative growth."[11] In our studies of childhood and sexuality, we have seen how this is so.

We have seen that, in the "pairings" of child and parent and of sexual partners, what is at stake is whether a subject is being recognized *as* such. Further, in each of these cases we have seen that this issue is not something that is engaged with primarily at the reflective, cognitive level, but is something "lived" at the practical, bodily, affective level: in both childhood development and sex, our recognition as subjects is what is defining the prereflective life that provides the "platform and character" of our explicit, "melodic" experiences. Furthermore, these prereflective structures of experience are in general *formative* for us: for the child, as we have seen, the intimacy of parental pairing shapes the child's lived sense of "I can"; for adults, our relations of erotic intimacy are typically analogously formative of our lived sense of ourselves.[12] It is in our intimate bonds, in other words, that the parameters for our lives as independent individuals are laid, and the more familiar matters of ethical action are thus circumscribed by the more basic question of the ethical dimensions of these founding parameters.

This, then, is the ultimate weight of the phenomenological description of the experience of others: it is phenomenology that precisely gives us the resources to look behind the simple, "melodic" terms of our familiar descriptions of the world to see the nonreflective ethical commitments that are definitive of the formative intersubjective bonds that are the implicit meaning of all of our perceptual life.

Notes

Chapter 1

1. See, for example, Husserl, *Ideas*, sections 27–30.
2. See Husserl's discussion of co-perception in *Thing and Space*, section 24.
3. See Husserl, *Analyses concerning Passive Synthesis*, 43, 48, and elsewhere, and *Thing and Space*, section 24. See also the discussion of actional and nonactional consciousness in section 35 of *Ideas*: "Every perception of a physical thing has, in this manner, a halo of *background-intuitions* (or background-seeings, in case one already includes in intuiting the advertedness to the really seen), and that is also a '*lived experience of consciousness*' or, more briefly, 'consciousness,' and, more particularly, '*of* all that which in fact lies in the objective 'background' seen along with it" (70, italics his, modified Kersten translation).
4. See *Ideas*, 94–95. See also *Analyses concerning Passive Synthesis*, 42, 43, 48, 266, and *Thing and Space*, section 18.
5. See section 41 of *Ideas*. See also *Analyses concerning Passive Synthesis*, sections 1–3, and *Thing and Space*, sections 14–17.
6. Husserl, *Ideas*, 87, modified Kersten translation.
7. Husserl, *Ideas*, 92.
8. See, for example, Husserl, *Analyses concerning Passive Synthesis*, 43, 44, 48, and elsewhere.
9. Husserl, *Ideas*, 95.
10. Ibid., 94, modified Kersten translation.
11. See also Husserl, *Cartesian Meditations*, section 19 and *Analyses concerning Passive Synthesis*, sections 1–3. For additional discussion of the horizon structure of perceptual experience, see Held, "Husserl's Phenomenological Method," particularly 13–17, and Held, "Husserl's Phenomenology of the Life World," particularly 37–40; Costello, *Layers in Husserl's Phenomenology*, 12–22; and Ihde, *Experimental Phenomenology*, 35–44. Husserl argues that an object's horizons imply the world as horizon; see Welton, *The Other Husserl*, particularly, 70–95, 331–46.

12. Husserl, *Ideas*, 91.

13. Ibid., 89.

14. Husserl, *Cartesian Meditations*, 33, italics his. See also Husserl, *Ideas*, section 84. For a technical discussion of what Husserl means by "intentionality," see Lampert, *Synthesis and Backwards Reference*, 1–11, especially 2. See also Sartre's excellent discussion in *Being and Nothingness*, 11–17.

15. See Husserl, *Ideas*, section 44: "[T]he indeterminacies become more precisely determined and are themselves eventually converted into clearly given determinations; conversely, to be sure, the clear is changed again into the unclear, the presented into the non-presented, etc. *To be in infinitum imperfect in this manner is part of the unannullable essence of the correlation between 'physical thing' and perception of a physical thing*" (94, italics his). See also Husserl, *Thing and Space*, section 39.

16. "It can already be seen universally that, no matter what its genus may be, the being of something transcendent, understood as a being *for* an Ego, can become given only in a manner analogous to that in which a physical thing is given, therefore through appearances" (*Ideas*, 95, italics his). See also *Thing and Space*, section 6: "The perception which stands before my eyes, and on which I exercise phenomenological reduction, is an absolute givenness; I possess it, as it were, for itself, with all that essentially makes it up. It is 'immanent.' The intentional object, however, is precisely 'transcendent'" (15).

17. Merleau-Ponty, *Phenomenology of Perception*, 100/74, italics his.

18. Husserl, *Analyses concerning Passive Synthesis*, 41.

19. Ibid., 42. See also Husserl's discussion of adequate perception in, for example, *Thing and Space*, sections 32–33. See Lampert, *Synthesis and Backyard Reference*, 73–87, for a discussion of related descriptions in Husserl's *Logical Investigations*.

20. Russon makes a similar point in *Bearing Witness*: "[S]ense and action are not separable: perception is a kind of acting, a bodily answering to a call that allows something to be realized" (14).

21. See Merleau-Ponty's discussion of the "human order" in *The Structure of Behavior*, 160–84, and his "Introduction" to the *Phenomenology of Perception* in which he writes: "Normal functioning must be understood as a process of integration in which the text of the external world is not copied, but constituted" (9). This insight is critical to the "enactive" approach within the cognitive sciences; see, for example, Varela, Thompson, and Rosch, *The Embodied Mind*; Noë, *Action in Perception*; and Thompson, *Mind and Life*. For a discussion of the enactive approach and Merleau-Ponty's work, see Marratto, *The Intercorporeal Self*, 11–38.

22. Thus, Merleau-Ponty, while affirming the concept of *Gestalt*, argues that this concept must be understood existentially (*Phenomenology of Perception*, 71–77/47–51).

23. Merleau-Ponty, *Phenomenology of Perception*, 249/213.

24. For this reason, a person who cannot walk up and down them will experience the stairs, not as the building's entrance or exit, but actually as an obstacle to entering or exiting the building. For a discussion of how a loss of mobility changes the character of the perceived world, see Toombs, "The Lived Experience of Disability." On how Merleau-Ponty's work can continue to contribute to work in disability studies, as well as critical race theory and feminist theory, see Weiss, "The Normal, the Natural, the Normative."

25. Heidegger, *Being and Time*, 69: "What everyday dealings are initially busy with is not tools themselves, but the work. What is to be produced in each case is what is primarily taken care of and thus also what is at hand. The work bears the totality of references in which useful things are encountered."

26. Thus, Merleau-Ponty refers to both a "motor signification" and a "motor intentionality" (*Phenomenology of Perception*, 140/112 ff.).

27. Merleau-Ponty, *Phenomenology of Perception*, 125–130/101–3, 176–177/142–143. On the body schema as a tacit awareness of one's body, see also Morris, *The Sense of Space*, 33–52, and Russon, "The Spatiality of Self-Consciousness." For a discussion of the distinction between body image and body schema, see Gallagher, *How the Body Shapes the Mind*, 17–64.

28. Merleau-Ponty, *Phenomenology of Perception*, 135/108.

29. Ibid., 171/139. Merleau-Ponty draws on Husserl here; see Husserl, *Cartesian Mediations*, 97, and *Ideas II*, 159. While Carman, for example, argues that Husserl and Merleau-Ponty's conceptions of the body are profoundly different insofar as Merleau-Ponty understands the body as constitutive of intentionality and Husserl does not, Costello argues that Husserl's notion of "overlaying" entails a conception of the body as constitutive of intentionality. See, Carman, "The Body" and Costello, *Layers*, 163. On the relation between Husserl and Merleau-Ponty's conceptions of the body, see also Zahavi, "Merleau-Ponty on Husserl," 15–20.

30. Heidegger, *Being and Time*, section 16; "world is something 'in which' [*worin*] Dasein as a being always already was, and the world is that to which Dasein can always only come back whenever it explicitly moves toward something in some way. According to our foregoing interpretation, being-in-the-world signifies the unthematic, circumspect absorption in the references constitutive for the handiness of the totality of useful things. Taking care of things always already occurs on the basis of a familiarity with the world" (75, italics his).

31. See Russon, *Sites of Exposure*, 35–44.

32. Merleau-Ponty, *Phenomenology of Perception*, 182/147.

33. For a discussion of how our handling of things speaks to our way of having a world and our larger commitments, see Russon, *Human Experience*, particularly 84–121.

34. For description and analysis of the basic phenomenon of the phantom limb, see Ramachandran and Blakeslee, *Phantoms in the Brain*. For rich discussions of Merleau-Ponty's analysis of the phantom limb, see Jacobson, "Neglecting

Space"; Russon, "Haunted by History" and "The Impossibilities of the I"; and Talero, "Merleau-Ponty and the Bodily Subject of Learning."

35. Merleau-Ponty, *Phenomenology of Perception*, 105/79: "The phenomenon in fact depends on 'psychical' determinants. A phantom limb appears for a subject not previously experiencing one when an emotion or situation evokes those of the injury."

36. Merleau-Ponty, *Phenomenology of Perception*, 110/83: "This phenomenon—distorted by both physiological and psychological explanations—can nevertheless be understood from the perspective of being in the world." See also Merleau-Ponty, *Phenomenology of Perception*, 106–9/80–82.

37. Talero, "Merleau-Ponty and the Bodily Subject of Learning," 193.

38. For related discussions of perceptual experience as a form of learning, see Howell, "Learning and the Development of Meaning"; Morris, *The Sense of Space*, 93–100; and Bredlau, "Learning to See."

39. *Phenomenology of Perception*, 111–112/84–85: "[I]t is as though our body comprises two distinct layers, that of the habitual body and that of the actual body. . . . [M]y body must be grasped not merely in an instantaneous, singular, and full experience, but moreover under an aspect of generality and as an impersonal being."

40. Talero, "Merleau-Ponty and the Bodily Subject of Learning," 93.

41. For further discussion of habit and other forms of bodily memory, see Casey, "Habitual Body and Memory in Merleau-Ponty" and *Remembering*, 146–80.

42. Russon, *Bearing Witness*, 11.

43. Ibid. On the theme of openness in Russon's earlier work, *Human Experience*, see Morris, "The Open Figure." Morris argues that the themes of openness and figure that Russon develops in *Human Experience* "resonate with recent developments in science" (316), including studies of touch (317–19) and mirror neurons (322–23).

44. Russon, *Bearing Witness*, 14.

45. Ibid., 19.

46. Ibid., 17–18.

47. Ibid., 19.

48. Ibid.

49. Ibid.

50. Compare Russon, *Sites of Exposure*, 35–36, on the inconspicuous, familiar context that defines our "home."

51. Russon uses the term "polytemporality" to describe the way in which music does not have a simple or single form of temporal flow; see *Bearing Witness*, 18.

52. Russon, *Bearing Witness*, 21.

53. See Russon, *Sites of Exposure*, 41–42, for examples of the variety of different experiences that can count as "being at home."

54. Russon, *Bearing Witness*, 15.

55. Ibid.

56. Compare Russon, *Sites of Exposure*, 42–43: "We assume our own developed identities by adopting these . . . particularities *as* proper, *as* normative for how things should be, and we live within the character and from the platform they provide for our engagement with ourselves, with our family members, with our other companions, and with the larger world."

Chapter 2

1. For a full development of this theme of perceptual attention and freedom, see Russon, "Freedom and Passivity"; on the distinctive nature of subjectivity, see Russon, *Sites of Exposure*, chapter 1.

2. On the interpretation of Descartes, see, for example, Aramides, *Other Minds*, and Baker and Morris, *Descartes' Dualism*.

3. Reddy, *How Infants Know Minds*, 10.

4. For a brief overview of these two theories, see Reddy, *How Infants Know Minds*, particularly 18–25, and Gallagher, "The Practice of Mind."

5. For a discussion of the role of theory of mind theory in research on mutual gaze and social cognition, see Stawarska, "Mutual Gaze and Social Cognition." See also Zahavi, *Subjectivity and Selfhood*, 179–222.

6. As Reddy writes, "Both first-person and third-person routes see the knowledge of other minds as an attributional process—something which requires more than just perceiving the psychological" (*How Infants Know Minds*, 25). Merleau-Ponty also discusses, and rejects, a process of attribution as the basis for our experience of other people; see, for example, *Phenomenology of Perception*, 409/367–68, and "The Child's Relations with Others," 246–47.

7. Husserl, *Cartesian Meditations*, 112 ff.

8. As Husserl writes in *Ideas*, "The spatial physical thing which we see is, with all its transcendence, still something perceived, given 'in person' in the manner peculiar to consciousness. It is not the case that, in its stead, a picture or a sign is given. A picture-consciousness or a sign-consciousness must not be substituted for perception" (92). See also Husserl, *Analyses concerning Passive Synthesis*, 55: "Adumbrating, exhibiting in data of sensation, is totally different from an interpretation through signs." For discussion of the prevalence of representationalist conceptions of perception, see Thompson, *Mind in Life*; Varela, Thompson, and Rosch, *The Embodied Mind*; Noë, *Action in Perception*; Bredlau, "Monstrous Faces"; and Taylor, "Merleau-Ponty and the Epistemological Picture."

9. See, for example, Merleau-Ponty's criticisms of Pavlov in *The Structure of Behavior*, 52–93; see also Merleau-Ponty, *The Structure of Behavior*, 127: "[T]he essential feature of the phenomenon [of behavior], the paradox which is constitutive of it: behavior is not a thing, but neither is it an idea." On the "ontological shift" (213) that the scientific results Merleau-Ponty discusses in *The Structure of Behavior* require, see Barbaras, "A Phenomenology of Life." On the broader conception of nature entailed by Merleau-Ponty's conception of behavior, see Bannon, *From Mastery to Mystery*, 97–152.

10. Heidegger, *Being and Time*, 74. Although Heidegger refers to an actual workshop on 70 and 82, on 74 he uses the term more broadly to refer to the world as the site of our projects: "This circumspect noticing of the reference to the particular what-for makes the what-for visible and with it the context of the work, the whole 'workshop' as that in which taking care has already been dwelling."

11. See, for example, Husserl's discussion of the lived body in *Ideas II*, particularly section 18a–b and Merleau-Ponty's discussion of bodily intentionality in *Phenomenology of Perception*, particularly 140–42/112–14, 154–56/124–26, and 172–73/523–25 (endnote 99).

12. Husserl, *Cartesian Meditations*, 119.

13. On Husserl's conception of the body and its role in the experience of other people, see Zahavi, *Husserl's Phenomenology*, 98–125.

14. Husserl, *Cartesian Meditations*, 119.

15. On Husserl's notion of appresentation and how appresentation with respect to physical objects differs from appresentation with respect to people, see Carr, *Phenomenology and the Problem of History*, 84–99.

16. This broader sense of orientation is reflected in Husserl's description of consciousness as an "I can" (*Cartesian Meditations*, 97; *Ideas II*, 159; and elsewhere). See also Gibson's description in *The Ecological Approach to Perception* of living organisms as perceiving the "affordances" of their environment and Morris's discussion of orientation as having a "concernful and emotional aspect" (144) in *The Sense of Space*, 144–58.

17. For phenomenological accounts of the experience of being at home in the world that resonate with this richer understanding of orientation, see Jacobson, "Agoraphobia and Hypochondria as Disorders of Dwelling" and "A Developed Nature"; McMahon, "Home Invasions"; Steinbock, *Home and Beyond*, particularly 186–235; and Russon, *Sites of Exposure*, 35–60.

18. Heidegger, *Being and Time*, 104.

19. Merleau-Ponty, *Phenomenology of Perception*, 332/293 ff.

20. Ibid., 338/299.

21. Husserl, *Cartesian Meditations*, 112 ff.

22. See Costello, *Layers in Husserl's Phenomenology*, particularly 29–47, for a more detailed discussion of Husserl's "pairing" relation. For further discussion

of the role of the body in the "pairing" relation, see Zahavi, "Empathy and Mirroring," particularly 234–41; Biceaga, *The Concept of Passivity*, 95–109; and Dodd, *Idealism and Corporeity*, 8–37.

23. Husserl, *Cartesian Meditations*, 113 ff.

24. One could still argue that what we experience as immediate could nonetheless be mediated by unconscious processes. Yet once we begin to invoke unconscious processes, we are no longer describing our experience but, instead, explaining it, and the question is whether such an explanation is even necessary. As Reddy writes, "there is an alternative which starts from questioning the very assumption of a profound gap between minds" (*How Infants Know Minds*, 25).

25. Merleau-Ponty's discussion of illusion in the *Phenomenology of Perception* is helpful for thinking through this idea; he writes, "Each perception, though always potentially 'crossed out' and pushed over to the realm of illusions, only disappears in order to leave place for another perception that corrects it" (402/359–60).

26. For a discussion of Merleau-Ponty's account of our perception of others in light of the problem of other minds, see Hass, *Merleau-Ponty's Philosophy*, 100–112.

27. Merleau-Ponty, *Phenomenology of Perception*, 411/370. See also Merleau-Ponty's chapter "The Intertwining—The Chiasm" in *The Visible and the Invisible*, in which he makes reference, for example, to "an intercorporeal being" (143), his discussion of "co-perception" in "The Philosopher and His Shadow" (*Signs*, 170), and his description of others existing "as outlines, deviations, and variants of a single Vision in which I too participate" in the "Introduction" of *Signs* (15). Likewise, he suggests that just as each person's sense organs have a shared perception of the world, so, too, do we share perception with other people. For further helpful discussion of these themes in Merleau-Ponty's work, see Maclaren, "Intercorporeality, Intersubjectivity," particularly 189–93, and Marratto, *The Intercorporeal Self*, particularly 141–63.

28. See, for example, Merleau-Ponty's discussion of constancy of form and size, *Phenomenology of Perception*, 352–58/312–18: "[E]very attitude of my body is immediately from me the power for a certain spectacle, because each spectacle is for me what it is within a certain kinesthetic situation, and because, in other words, my body is permanently stationed in front of things in order to perceive them and, inversely, appearances are always enveloped for me within a certain bodily attitude. Thus, if I know the relation from appearance to the kinesthetic situation, this is not through a law or from a formula, but rather insofar as I have a body and insofar as I am, through this body, geared into a world" (356/316).

29. I agree with Marratto that "the body schema is constitutively intercorporeal and, as such, it is not a simple self-identity. The body schema subtends a proper body insofar as it also disappropriates it. The body schema makes space for a body proper insofar as it has already made space for otherness" (*The

Intercorporeal Self, 159). Marratto argues that Dillon's conception of intersubjectivity as "involving a 'transfer of corporeal schema,'" Gallagher's conception of the body schema as including "physiological processes subtending conscious appearance," and Zahavi's conception of body self-awareness as an "originary first-personal givenness of bodily self-experience" (154) are all inadequate insofar as they understand the unity of the body as a simple self-identity rather than as an "expressive unity—it is accomplished as a sense in movement attesting to the unity of my body but it bears an attestation of the unreflective, anonymous prehistory of this unity" (153). On Dillon's conception of the body schema, see *Merleau-Ponty's Ontology*, 113–29; on Gallagher's conception of the body schema, see *How the Body Shapes the Mind*, 40–64; and on Zahavi's conception of bodily self-awareness, see *Self-Awareness and Alterity*, 91–109.

30. Maclaren describes this perception of other bodies' perceptivity as an "inhabitation or shadowing of other's actions" ("Intercorporeality, Intersubjectivity," 190).

31. Merleau-Ponty, *Phenomenology of Perception*, 410/368.

32. The subject who perceives the world as, for example, visible is thus not so much an "I," a consciousness distinct from every other consciousness, but a "one," a consciousness that belongs to any body with seeing eyes. The perception of the world as visible is shared rather than private; we perceive as a member of the group of those who have seeing eyes rather than as solitary individuals. Of course, most of our adult perceptual experience is not simply an experience of color or sound as such, but, instead, an experience of a more personally significant situation. Nonetheless, this personal significance, Merleau-Ponty argues, is founded upon an impersonal significance. I can only see the stop sign, for example, as a stop sign insofar as it is experienced as visible and as having two different colors. The more personal meanings the world has for a person, therefore, reflect more generic meanings that did not begin, and will not end, with this one person's perceptual consciousness. Thus, our perception of the world as, for example, visible and audible, is not, in an important sense, our own doing. Although our perception of specific colors and sounds requires practice, our perception of color and sound as such does not. Rather, we have the ability to see color as such because we are born with eyes and the ability to hear sound as such because we are born with ears.

33. Thus, Maclaren distinguishes between intercorporeality and intersubjectivity, while also arguing that they are two moments of a single phenomenon ("Intercorporeality, Intersubjectivity," 189). On the relation between the experience of a shared world and an asymmetry between our experience and other's experience, see also Carman, *Merleau-Ponty*, 142–49.

34. Merleau-Ponty, *The Structure of Behavior*, 169. See also Merleau-Ponty's discussion of a spectator at a soccer game ("The Child's Relations with Others,"

145). For an excellent discussion of the implications of this discussion for our understanding of the experience of others, see Maclaren, "Intercorporeality, Intersubjectivity," 189–93.

35. This situation is similar to the situation Merleau-Ponty describes of a child who perceives adults engaged in sexual activity: "If a child accidentally witnesses a sexual scene, he can understand it without having the experience of desire of the bodily attitudes that it expresses, but if the child has not yet reached the degree of maturity at which this behavior becomes a possibility for him, then the sexual scene will remain merely an unusual and disturbing spectacle, it will not make sense" (*Phenomenology of Perception*, 225/190). The child perceives the adults as perceptive, and yet she does not perceive the meaning that each adult's body has for the other. Insofar as her body is not yet capable of gearing into the world in the same way as a sexually mature adult, the child does not yet perceive the world as sexually significant. This theme of the sexual dimension of bodily life is the subject of chapter 4.

36. As Maclaren writes, "The other's behavior therefore opens us up to the meanings of things. But it does more; it also sets up a situation in which we feel called upon to actively consolidate those meanings for ourselves" ("Intercorporeality, Intersubjectivity," 191).

37. On this point and its implications for our experience of other people, see Zahavi, *Husserl and Transcendental Intersubjectivity*, 149–59.

38. Merleau-Ponty, *Phenomenology of Perception*, 410/369.

39. Ibid., 409/367.

40. Heidegger, *Being and Time*, 116: "The world of Dasein is a *with-world* [*Mitwelt*]. Being-in is *being-with* [*Mitsein*] others. The innerworldly being-in-itself of others is *Dasein-with* [*Mitdasein*]" (italics his).

41. Russon, *Bearing Witness to Epiphany*, 114.

42. Compare McMahon's discussion, in "Home Invasions," of the way that, just as we can care for others by caring for their things, so can we violate others by violating their things. See also Russon, *Bearing Witness*, 107–8.

43. Russon, *Human Experience*, 91. Russon identifies this ideal of normalcy with a stoic conception of the self: "What the stoic conception of agency misrepresents is precisely this: its embeddedness in and contextualization by *essentially* 'non-stoic' dimensions of our personality, that is, dimensions in which we do not have self-conscious insight and do not exercise self-control. An attempt to force a stoic mould onto our life (whether in theory or in behavior), runs afoul of the inherent nature of that very life, inverting cause and effect" ("The Virtue of Stoicism," 351).

44. For additional explication of Russon's conception of neurosis and the ideal of normalcy as itself neurotic, see Marratto, "Russon's Pharmacy," 114–16.

45. Russon, *Human Experience*, 92.

46. Ibid., 93.

47. On Russon's phenomenological interpretation of family life, see Jacobson, "The Body as Family Life," 50–52.

48. *Human Experience*, 94.

49. Ibid., 98–100. See also Jacobson's conception of the "eating disorder" of anorexia ("The Interpersonal Expression of Human Spatiality") and Maclaren's conception of the "emotional disorder" of alexthymia ("Emotional Disorder and the Mind-Body Problem") as habitual modes of intersubjective behavior.

50. *Human Experience*, 87.

Chapter 3

1. See, for example, Husserl, "The Origin of Geometry" and *Ideas I*, chapters 5 and 8. For Merleau-Ponty's use of this notion, see "Indirect Language and the Voices of Silence," 59; this concept is also broadly discussed throughout Merleau-Ponty's works "Course Notes: Husserl at the Limits of Phenomenology" and *Institution and Passivity*. For a rich discussion of this concept within the context of Merleau-Ponty's philosophy, see Beith, *The Birth of Sense*, introduction, section 4, and chapter 2, section 4.

2. Merleau-Ponty, *Phenomenology of Perception*, 409/368.

3. Merleau-Ponty, "The Child's Relations with Others." 115–17.

4. Merleau-Ponty, *Phenomenology of Perception*, 409/368.

5. See, for example, Courage et al., "Variability in the Early Development of Visual Self-Recognition."

6. On Merleau-Ponty's account of infants' mirroring of others' actions, see also Maclaren, "Intercorporeality, Intersubjectivity," and Welsh, *The Child as Natural Phenomenologist*, 45–71. For a discussion of mirroring in general in Merleau-Ponty's work, see Al-Saji, "Vision, Mirror and Expression."

7. Heidegger, *Being and Time*, 176. See also Heidegger, *Being and Time*, 177: "Existentially, a state-of-mind implies a disclosive submission to the world, out of which we can encounter something that matters to us."

8. Russon, *Human Experience*, 44.

9. For further discussion of Merleau-Ponty's conception of space as traced out by affective trajectories, see Jacobson, "Agoraphobia and Hypochondria" and "The Gift of Memory," and Bredlau, "A Respectful World."

10. On the collective realization necessary to play, see Gadamer, *Truth and Method*, particularly 102–14, and Dewey, *Experience and Education*, particularly 51–60, and *Democracy and Education*, particularly 31–38.

11. Merleau-Ponty makes a similar point in his discussion of Guillaume and the problem of imitation. See, "Consciousness and the Acquisition of Language," 32–40.

12. Welsh offers an extended appraisal of Merleau-Ponty's claims about infant experience in light of contemporary psychological research in *The Child as Natural Phenomenologist*, 72–105.

13. Meltzoff and Moore, "Newborn Infants Imitate Adult Facial Gestures."

14. Gallagher, *How the Body Shapes the Mind*, 83.

15. Ibid., 84.

16. Earlier in his discussion of neonate imitation, Gallagher writes, "The infant, faced with novel motor and gestural activities, has the capacity to act out what it sees in the face of the adult—it recognizes what it sees as one of its own capabilities" (*How the Body Shapes the Mind*, 75), and he argues that infants are able to know "pre-reflectively, in the very act of gesturing, whether the gesture is on target or not" (*How the Body Shapes the Mind*, 74). It is not clear here, though, whether Gallagher is using the term "gesture" in the same sense as Merleau-Ponty, as a perceptive movement that is a way of having a world, or in a more ordinary sense, as a perceived movement that is a movement within the world.

17. I have discussed this theme further in "Perceiving through Another: Incorporation and the Child Perceiver."

18. See, for example, Scaife and Bruner, "The Capacity for Joint Visual Attention," and Morales et al., "Gaze Following."

19. Stawarska, "Mutual Gaze and Social Cognition."

20. On the philosophical implications of Stern's work, see also Zahavi, *Self-Awareness and Alterity*, 164–90, and Willett, *Maternal Ethics*, 24–30.

21. Stern, *The First Relationship*, 34.

22. Ibid., 100.

23. For additional discussion of affect regulation, see Stern, *The Interpersonal World of the Infant*, 89–90, 101–4. See also Willett, *Interspecies Ethics*, 88–98.

24. Stern, *The First Relationship*, 113.

25. Admittedly, Stern's own conception of affect as a "subjective feeling that cannot be observed or even directly tapped in a nonverbal infant" rather than as a way of having a world seems to prevent Stern from recognizing the full extent of the collaboration between infant and caregiver (*The First Relationship*, 83).

26. Feinman, "In the Broad Valley," 4.

27. Bretherton, "Social Referencing," 58.

28. See Trevarthen, "Descriptive Analyses." For a brief discussion of Trevarthen's distinction between primary and secondary intersubjectivity, see Reddy, *How Infants Know Minds*, 71–72.

29. Reddy, *How Infants Know Minds*, 27, italics hers.

30. For a more detailed account of the second-person approach, including its three core features, see Reddy, *How Infants Know Minds*, particularly 26–27.

31. See, for example, Reddy, *How Infants Know Minds*, 45–54, 74–82.

32. See, for example, Costall, "Things That Help," and Rossmanith, et al., "Joint Structuring of Shared Spaces."
33. Stern, *The First Relationship*, 97.
34. Ibid., 18, 49–68.
35. Ibid., 11.
36. Ibid.
37. Ibid., 80.
38. Ibid., 84.
39. Ibid., 17.
40. Ibid., 4.
41. Ibid., 63, 81, 121.
42. Ibid., 72 ("dance"), and 85, 86, 92, 110 ("like a dance").
43. Ibid., 57.
44. Ibid., 85.
45. For a powerful description of the relation between mother and nursing infant as a kind of dance, see Simms, "Milk and Flesh," particularly 26–30.
46. Stern, *The First Relationship*, 113.
47. See Sartre's discussion of the gaze in *Being and Nothingness*, 347–34.
48. Carr et al., "Mother-Infant Attachment."
49. Ibid., 337.
50. Sorce and Emde, "Mother's Presence," 739.
51. Ibid., 740.
52. Ibid., 744.
53. Ibid.
54. Ibid.
55. Ibid., 738.
56. Ibid., 739.
57. Carr et al., "Mother-Infant Attachment," 337.
58. That a pairing sustained by language rather than vision is, nonetheless, less preferable to infants could be due the limited language skills of 18- to 30-month-old infants.
59. Sorce et al., "Maternal Emotional Signaling."
60. De Jaegher and Di Paolo, "Participatory sense-making," 497.
61. Ibid., 498.
62. Stern, *The First Relationship*, 114.
63. De Jaegher and Di Paolo, "Participatory Sense-Making," 499.
64. Stern, *The First Relationship*, 94.
65. Ibid., 96.
66. De Jaegher and Di Paolo, "Participatory Sense-Making," 493.
67. Indeed, infants cannot insure that others will interact with them at all. For a phenomenological account of the impact of severe neglect on infants, see Simms, "Intimacy and the Face of the Other."

68. On the impact of others' perception on the child's sense of self, see Maclaren, "Embodied Perception of Others."
69. Russon, "Between Two Intimacies," 65.
70. Ibid.
71. Russon, *Human Experience*, 62. Of course, this cooperation may be extremely underdeveloped (Russon, *Human Experience*, 54); the child is not in a position to recognize the situation as cooperative, and her cooperation may simply entail submitting to the demands of her family.
72. Russon, *Human Experience*, 65.
73. Russon, "Between Two Intimacies," 66.
74. Ibid., italics his.
75. Russon, "Virtues of Agency," 167.
76. Ibid., 170.
77. Beauvoir, *The Second Sex*, 283–340. See also Iris Marion Young, "Throwing like a Girl."
78. Russon, "Virtues of Agency," 169.
79. Laing refers to this sense as "ontological security" (*The Divided Self*, 39 ff).
80. Russon, "Between Two Intimacies," 67.
81. Russon, "Virtues of Agency," 169.
82. Ibid., 168.
83. Ibid., 167.
84. Ibid., 171.
85. Ibid.
86. Ibid.
87. Ibid., 174.
88. Russon, "Between Two Intimacies," 67.
89. Russon, *Human Experience*, 65.
90. Russon, "Between Two Intimacies," 67, italics his.
91. On this point, see Russon's discussion of property (*Bearing Witness to Epiphany*, 95–105).

Chapter 4

1. For a rich discussion of the impersonal dimension to our intersubjective experience, see Russon, *Sites of Exposure*, 44–49, for the basic phenomenological difference between personal and impersonal interactions, and 65–100, for the way in which the impersonal "environment of indifference" plays an essential role in our personal and political lives.
2. Russon, *Human Experience*, 70.
3. Russon, "Between Two Intimacies," 67.

4. Russon, *Human Experience*, 68, italics his.

5. I will focus on Merleau-Ponty's discussion of desire in the *Phenomenology of Perception*, although he does make reference to desire in *The Visible and the Invisible*. For a discussion of desire in this later work, see Barbaras, *The Being of the Phenomenon*, 267–79.

6. Merleau-Ponty, *Phenomenology of Perception*, 533/156.

7. Ibid., 194/159. On this point, see also Salamon, *Assuming a Body*, 50–55.

8. Merleau-Ponty, *Phenomenology of Perception*, 205/170. On the relation between shame and Merleau-Ponty's account of erotic life, see Steinbock, "Erotic Perception."

9. For discussion of this case, see Lewis and Staehler, *Phenomenology: An Introduction*, 170–72. For a recent summary and discussion of some aspects of this case and its subsequent interpretation, see Marotta and Behrmann, "Patient Schn."

10. Merleau-Ponty, *Phenomenology of Perception*, 193/158.

11. Ibid.

12. For additional discussion of the implications of Schneider's sexual experience for Merleau-Ponty's account of sexuality, see Steinbock, "Erotic Perception," 175–86.

13. Merleau-Ponty, *Phenomenology of Perception*, 205/170.

14. Russon, *Bearing Witness to Epiphany*, 73. Russon differentiates this sexual form of finding ourselves "already" involved with another from the child's experience of already being "with" her parents, arguing for both the importance and the significantly different norms that govern these two forms of "intimacy" in "Between Two Intimacies." He develops parallel themes in both *Bearing Witness to Epiphany* and *Human Experience*. While immersed in family life, we tend not to notice the otherness of those who belong to our family: "As family members we tend to live as if we formed a single fabric, as if for both of us there were an identical 'here'" (*Bearing Witness to Epiphany*, 74). In adult life, however, we are drawn toward those who are, precisely, not familiar; it is the very nonidentity of the other's "here" with our "here" that exerts a pull on us (*Bearing Witness to Epiphany*, 74–5); in erotic experience, we, in our singular embodied subjectivity, encounter others in their singular embodied subjectivity.

15. As Steinbock writes, "Erotic perception is what connects us as lived-bodies to other lived-bodies" ("Erotic Perception," 178).

16. Hegel, *Phenomenology of Spirit*, paragraphs 166–67. See Ciavatta, "Hegel on Desire's Knowledge," and Russon, *Infinite Phenomenology*, 107–25.

17. Hegel, *Phenomenology of Spirit*, paragraphs 167 and 174.

18. Ibid., paragraphs 168 and 175.

19. Ibid., paragraph 179. See Ciavatta, *Spirit, the Family, and the Unconscious*, 17–52, and Russon, *Reading Hegel's Phenomenology*, 59–69.

20. Hegel, *Phenomenology of Spirit*, paragraphs 186–89.
21. Ibid., paragraphs 190–96.
22. Ibid., paragraph 182.
23. Merleau-Ponty, *Phenomenology of Perception*, 205/170.
24. Although Sartre also offers a rich phenomenological account of sexual life in *Being and Nothingness*, I think that Beauvoir's extended discussion of bodily habituation in the context of sexual life resonates particularly well with Merleau-Ponty's discussion of sexuality. On the relation between Beauvoir and Merleau-Ponty's conceptions of the body and sexuality, see Heinämaa, "Simone de Beauvoir's Phenomenology of Sexual Difference" and *Toward a Phenomenology of Sexual Difference*. Heinämaa argues that "the philosophical context in which Beauvoir operated is the phenomenology of the body that Edmund Husserl initiated and Maurice Merleau-Ponty further developed" ("Simone de Beauvoir's Phenomenology," 20).
25. Beauvoir, *The Second Sex*, 383.
26. My choice of the term "expressive" reflects Beauvoir's description of the penis as, "like the hand or the face, the imperious expression of a subjectivity" (*The Second Sex*, 392) and resonates with Merleau-Ponty's description of the body as expressive (*Phenomenology of Perception*, 213–41/179–205. As I will argue, expression is not, in principle, imperious, although it may certainly be so in practice.
27. Beauvoir, *The Second Sex*, 283–340. For a discussion of Merleau-Ponty's conception of women's embodiment, see Welsh, "The Developing Body."
28. On the idea that women are habituated to experience their bodies in terms of an "I cannot," see also Young, "Throwing like a Girl."
29. Beauvoir, *The Ethics of Ambiguity*, 37.
30. Beauvoir, *The Second Sex*, 397.
31. Ibid., 398.
32. Beauvoir, *The Ethics of Ambiguity*, 37. For further discussion of this idea, see Bredlau, "Simone de Beauvoir's Apprenticeship of Freedom."
33. Beauvoir, *The Second Sex*, 391.
34. Ibid., 389.
35. Ibid., 384.
36. Ibid., 406.
37. We do not need to consciously choose to pursue domination in the contact between our bodies and others' to actually pursue such domination.
38. Beauvoir, *The Second Sex*, 411.
39. See Russon, "Why Sexuality Matters."
40. Merleau-Ponty, *Phenomenology of Perception*, 206/170. On the simultaneous activity and passivity of the body, see Maclaren, "Touching Matters," 97–101.
41. See Merleau-Ponty's discussion of the reversibility of touching and touched in *The Visible and the Invisible* and Morris, "The Enigma of Reversibility."

42. Russon offers a very similar description of touch in *Bearing Witness*, 75–82. See also Russon, *Sites of Exposure*, 49–50.

43. Merleau-Ponty, "Man Seen from the Outside," 89; *Phenomenology of Perception*, 205/170.

44. As Bergoffen writes, "In entering the opening of generous intersubjectivity, men and women allow themselves to be guided by the generosities of the erotic event. They embrace their capacities for active passivity and take up the risks of the flesh, the gift, and the bond" (Simone Beauvoir: (Re)counting the Sexual Difference, 264).

45. Merleau-Ponty, *Phenomenology of Perception*, 194/159.

46. Russon, *Bearing Witness*, 91.

47. Ibid., 94.

48. Russon, "Why Sexuality Matters," 42.

49. Russon, *Human Experience*, 108.

50. Russon, *Bearing Witness*, 75. See also Russon, "Why Sexuality Matters," 43–44, and *Human Experience*, 110.

51. Russon, *Human Experience*, 109.

52. On Russon's conception of the erotic, see Murphy, "John Russon," 147–49.

53. Russon, *Human Experience*, 92.

54. Merleau-Ponty, "Man Seen from the Outside," 90.

55. Beauvoir, *The Second Sex*, 389, italics hers.

56. Russon, *Human Experience*, 110.

57. Beauvoir, *The Second Sex*, 415.

58. Ibid. On this point, see also Gothlin, "Beauvoir and Sartre," 137–42. Gothlin argues that Beauvoir's conception of erotic desire as irreducible to relations of domination and subordination distinguishes her conception of erotic desire from Sartre's.

59. On the implications of Beauvoir's conception of sexuality for our understanding of traditional gender norms, see Heinämaa, "Beauvoir's Phenomenology of Sexual Difference." On its implications for the tradition of marriage, see Bergoffen, "Marriage, Autonomy and the Feminine Protest." On Beauvoir's conception of gender, see Butler, "Sex and Gender."

60. Beauvoir, *The Second Sex*, 415.

61. Russon, "Why Sexuality Matters," 41. Compare *Human Experience*: "Perhaps I can only feel sexually comfortable on a mattress that lies directly on the floor, or only when my father is out of town; perhaps I can only have an orgasm if you are partially clothed" (110).

62. Beauvoir, *The Ethics of Ambiguity*, 73. See also Beauvoir, *The Ethics of Ambiguity*: "[I]t is not true that the recognition of the freedom of others limits my own freedom. . . . The existence of others as a freedom defines my situation and is even the condition of my own freedom" (91).

Conclusion

1. Levinas, *Totality and Infinity*, 195.
2. Ibid., 194.
3. Ibid., 199.
4. Ibid., 198.
5. Ibid., 199, italics in original.
6. Ibid., 203.
7. Beauvoir, *Ethics of Ambiguity*, 73.
8. Russon, *Bearing Witness to Epiphany*, 85.
9. Ibid., 82–83.
10. Ibid., 79.
11. Ibid., 82.
12. See Russon, "Between Two Intimacies," for comparison and differentiation of these two situations.

Bibliography

Al-Saji, Alia. "Vision, Mirror and Expression: The Genesis of the Ethical Body in Merleau-Ponty's Later Works." In *Interrogating Ethics: Embodying the Good in Merleau-Ponty*. Edited by James Hatley, Janice McLane, and Christian Diehm. Pittsburgh: Duquesne University Press, 2006, 39–63.

Aramides, Anita. *Other Minds*. London: Routledge, 2001.

Baker, Gordon, and Katherine J. Morris. *Descartes' Dualism*. London: Routledge, 1996.

Bannon, Bryan. *From Mastery to Mystery*. Athens: Ohio University Press, 2014.

Barbaras, Renaud. *The Being of the Phenomenon: Merleau-Ponty's Ontology*. Translated by Ted Toadvine and Leonard Lawlor. Bloomington: Indiana University Press, 2004.

———. "A Phenomenology of Life." In *The Cambridge Companion to Merleau-Ponty*. Edited by Taylor Carman and Mark B. Hansen. Cambridge: Cambridge University Press, 2005, 206–30.

Beauvoir, Simone de. *The Ethics of Ambiguity*. Translated by Bernard Frechtman. New York: Citadel, 1991.

———. *The Second Sex*. Translated by Constance Borde and Sheila Malovany-Chevallier. New York: Vintage Books, 2011.

Beith, Don. *The Birth of Sense: Merleau-Ponty's Philosophy of Generative Passivity*. Athens: Ohio University Press, 2018.

Bergoffen, Debra. "Marriage, Autonomy and the Feminine Protest." In *The Philosophy of Simone de Beauvoir*. Edited by Margaret Simons. Bloomington: Indiana University Press, 2006, 92–112.

———. "Simone de Beauvoir: (Re)counting the Sexual Difference." In *The Cambridge Companion to Simone de Beauvoir*. Edited by Claudia Card. Cambridge: Cambridge University Press, 2006, 248–65.

Biceaga, Victor. *The Concept of Passivity in Husserl's Phenomenology*. Dordrect: Springer, 2010.

Bredlau, Susan. "Learning to See: Merleau-Ponty and the Navigation of Terrains." *Chiasmi International* 8 (2006): 191–97.

———. "Monstrous Faces and a World Transformed: Merleau-Ponty, Dolezal, and the Enactive Approach on Vision Without Inversion of the Retinal Image." *Phenomenology and the Cognitive Sciences* 10.4 (2011): 481–98.

———. "Perceiving through Another: Incorporation and the Child Perceiver." In *Perception and Its Development in Merleau-Ponty's Phenomenology*. Edited by Kirsten Jacobsen and John Russon. Toronto: University of Toronto Press, 2017, 81–98.

———. "A Respectful World." *Human Studies* 33 (2010): 411–23.

———. "Simone de Beauvoir's Apprenticeship of Freedom." *Phaenex* 6.1 (2011): 42–63.

Bretherton, Inge. "Social Referencing, Intentional Communication, and the Interfacing of Minds in Infancy." In *Social Referencing and the Social Construction of Reality in Infancy*. Edited by Saul Feinman. New York: Plenum, 1992, 57–77.

Butler, Judith. "Sex and Gender in Simone de Beauvoir's Second Sex." *Yale French Studies* 72 (1986): 35–49.

Carman, Taylor. "The Body in Husserl and Merleau-Ponty." *Philosophical Topics* 27.2 (1999): 205–26.

———. *Merleau-Ponty*. New York: Routledge, 2008.

Carr, David. *Phenomenology and the Problem of History*. Evanston: Northwestern University Press, 1974.

Carr, Suzanne J., et al. "Mother-Infant Attachment: The Importance of the Mother's Visual Field." *Child Development* 46 (1975): 331–38.

Casey, Edward S. "Habitual Body and Memory in Merleau-Ponty." *Man and World* 17 (1984): 279–97.

———. *Remembering: A Phenomenological Study*. Bloomington: Indiana University Press, 1987.

Ciavatta, David. "Hegel on Desire's Knowledge." *Review of Metaphysics* 61.3 (2008): 527–54.

———. *Spirit, the Family, and the Unconscious in Hegel's Philosophy*. Albany: State University of New York Press, 2009.

Costall, A. "Things That Help Make Us What We Are." In *Understanding the Self and Others: Explorations in Intersubjectivity and Interobjectivity*. Edited by G. Sammut et al. Oxford: Wiley/Blackwell, 2013, 66–76.

Costello, Peter. *Layers in Husserl's Phenomenology*. Toronto: University of Toronto Press, 2012.

Courage, Mary L., et al. 2004. "Variability in the Early Development of Visual Self-Recognition." *Infant Behavior and Development* 27: 509–32.

De Jaegher, Hanne, and Ezequiel Di Paolo. "Participatory Sense-Making: An Enactive Approach to Social Cognition." *Phenomenology and the Cognitive Sciences* 6 (2007): 485–507.

Descartes, René. *Meditations on First Philosophy*. Translated by John Cottingham. Cambridge: Cambridge University Press, 1996.

Dewey, John. *Democracy and Education: The Middle Works of John Dewey, Vol. 9.* Carbondale: Southern Illinois University Press, 2008.

———. *Experience and Education.* New York: Free Press, 2015.

Dillon, M. C. *Merleau-Ponty's Ontology.* Evanston: Northwestern University Press, 1998.

Dodd, James. *Idealism and Corporeity: An Essay on the Problem of Body in Husserl's Phenomenology.* Dordrect: Kluwer, 1997.

Feinman, Saul. "In the Broad Valley: An Integrative Look at Social Referencing." In *Social Referencing and the Social Construction of Reality in Infancy.* Edited by Saul Feinman. New York: Plenum, 1992, 3–13.

Fillion, Réal. *Multicultural Dynamics and the Ends of History: Explorations in Kant, Hegel, and Marx.* Ottawa: University of Ottawa Press, 2008.

Gadamer, Hans-Georg. *Truth and Method.* Translated by Joel Weinsheimer and Donald G. Marshall. London: Bloomsbury, 2013.

Gallagher, Shaun. *How the Body Shapes the Mind.* Oxford: Clarendon, 2005.

———. "The Practice of Mind." *Journal of Consciousness Studies* 8 (2001): 83–108.

Gibson, James J. *The Ecological Approach to Perception.* Hillsdale: Lawrence Erlbaum Associates, 1986.

Gothlin, Eva. "Beauvoir and Sartre on Appeal, Desire and Ambiguity." In *The Philosophy of Simone de Beauvoir.* Edited by Margaret Simons. Bloomington: Indiana University Press, 2006, 132–45.

Hegel, G. W. F. *Phenomenology of Spirit.* Translated by A. V. Miller. Oxford: Oxford University Press, 1977.

Heidegger, Martin. *Being and Time.* Translated by Joan Stambaugh. Albany: State University of New York Press, 2010.

Heinämaa, Sara. "Simone de Beauvoir's Phenomenology of Sexual Difference." In *The Philosophy of Simone de Beauvoir.* Edited by Margaret Simons. Bloomington: Indiana University Press, 2006, 20–41.

———. *Toward a Phenomenology of Sexual Difference: Husserl, Merleau-Ponty, Beauvoir.* Lanham: Rowman and Littlefield, 2003.

Held, Klaus. "Husserl's Phenomenological Method." In *The New Husserl: A Critical Reader.* Edited by Donn Welton. Bloomington: Indiana University Press, 2003, 3–31.

———. "Husserl's Phenomenology of the Life World." In *The New Husserl: A Critical Reader.* Edited by Donn Welton. Bloomington: Indiana University Press, 2003, 32–64.

Howell, Whitney. "Learning and the Development of Meaning: Husserl and Merleau-Ponty on the Temporality of Perception and Habit." *The Southern Journal of Philosophy* 53 (2015): 311–37.

Husserl, Edmund. *Analyses Concerning Passive and Active Synthesis.* Translated by Anthony J. Steinbock. Boston: Kluwer, 2001.

———. *Cartesian Meditations.* Translated by Dorion Cairns. Boston: Kluwer, 1993.

———. *Ideas Pertaining to a Pure Phenomenology and to a Phenomenological Philosophy, First Book*. Translated by F. Kersten. Boston: Kluwer, 1998.

———. *Ideas Pertaining to a Pure Phenomenology and to a Phenomenological Philosophy, Second Book*. Translated by R. Rojcewicz and A. Schuwer. Boston: Kluwer, 1989.

———. "The Origin of Geometry." Translated by David Carr. In *Husserl and the Limits of Phenomenology*. Evanston: Northwestern University Press, 2002, 93–116.

———. *Thing and Space: Lectures of 1907*. Translated by Richard Rojcewicz. Boston: Kluwer, 1997.

Ihde, Don. *Experimental Phenomenology*. Albany: State University of New York Press, 2012.

Jacobson, Kirsten. "Agoraphobia and Hypochondria as Disorders of Dwelling." *International Studies in Philosophy* 36.2 (2004): 31–44.

———. "The Body as Family Narrative: Russon and the Education of the Soul." *Anekaant: A Journal of Polysemic Thought* 3 (2015): 49–57.

———. "A Developed Nature: A Phenomenological Account of the Experience of Home." *Continental Philosophy Review* 42.3 (2009): 355–73.

———. "The Gift of Memory: Sheltering the I." In *Time, Memory, Institution: Merleau-Ponty's New Ontology of Self*. Edited by David Morris and Kym Maclaren. Athens: Ohio University Press, 2015, 29–42.

———. "The Interpersonal Expression of Human Spatiality: A Phenomenological Interpretation of Anorexia Nervosa." *Chiasmi International* 8 (2006): 157–73.

———. "Neglecting Space: Making Sense of a Partial Loss of One's World through a Phenomenological Account of the Spatiality of Embodiment." In *Perception and Its Development in Merleau-Ponty's Phenomenology*. Edited by Kirsten Jacobsen and John Russon. Toronto: University of Toronto Press, 2017, 101–22.

Laing, R. D. *The Divided Self*. London: Penguin Books, 1965.

Lampert, Jay. *Synthesis and Backwards Reference in Husserl's Logical Investigations*. Dordrect: Kluwer, 1995.

Lawlor, Leonard. *Derrida and Husserl: The Basic Problem of Phenomenology*. Bloomington: Indiana University Press, 2002.

Lewis, Michael, and Tanja Staehler. *Phenomenology: An Introduction*. New York: Continuum, 2010.

Maclaren, Kym. "Embodied Perceptions of Others as a Condition of Selfhood?" *Journal of Consciousness Studies* 15.8 (2008): 63–93.

———. "Emotional Disorder and the Mind-Body Problem: A Case Study of Alexithymia." *Chiasmi International* 8 (2006): 139–55.

———. "The 'Entre Deux' of Emotions: Emotions as Institutions." In *Perception and Its Development in Merleau-Ponty's Phenomenology*. Edited by Kirsten

Jacobson and John Russon. Toronto: University of Toronto Press, 2017, 51–80.

———. "Intercorporeality, Intersubjectivity and the Problem of 'Letting Others Be.'" *Chiasmi International* 4 (2002): 187–210.

———. "Touching Matters." *Emotion, Space and Society* 13 (2014): 95–102.

Marotta, J. J., and M. Behrmann. "Patient Schn: Has Goldstein and Gelb's Case Withstood the Test of Time?" *Neuropsychologia* 42 (2004): 633–38.

Marratto, Scott. "Alterity and Expression in Merleau-Ponty: A Response to Levinas." In *Perception and Its Development in Merleau-Ponty's Phenomenology*. Edited by Kirsten Jacobson and John Russon. Toronto: University of Toronto Press, 2017, 242–50.

———. *The Intercorporeal Self*. Albany: State University of New York Press, 2010.

———. "Russon's Pharmacy: Desire, Philosophy, and the Ambiguity of 'Mental Health.'" In *Philosophical Apprenticeships: Contemporary Continental Philosophy in Canada*. Edited by Jay Lampert and Jason Robinson. Ottawa: University of Ottawa Press, 2009, 98–120.

McMahon, Laura. "Home Invasions: Phenomenological and Psychanalytic Reflections on Embodiment Relations, Vulnerability and Breakdown." *Journal of Speculative Philosophy* 28.3 (2014): 358–69.

Meltzoff, Andrew N., and M. Keith Moore. "Newborn Infants Imitate Adult Facial Gestures." *Child Development* 54 (1983): 702–9.

Merleau-Ponty, Maurice. "The Child's Relations with Others." In *The Primacy of Perception*. Translated by William Cobb. Evanston: Northwestern University Press, 2010, 96–155.

———. "Consciousness and the Acquisition of Language." In *Child Psychology and Pedagogy*. Translated by Talia Welsh. Evanston: Northwestern University Press, 2010, 3–67.

———. "Indirect Language and the Voices of Silence." In *Signs*. Translated by Richard C. McCleary. Evanston: Northwestern University Press, 1998, 39–83.

———. *Institution and Passivity: Course Notes from the Collège de France (1954–1955)*. Translated by Leonard Lawlor and Heath Massey. Evanston: Northwestern University Press, 2010.

———. "Introduction." In *Signs*. Translated by Richard C. McCleary. Evanston: Northwestern University Press, 1998, 3–35.

———. "Man Seen from the Outside." In *The World of Perception*. Translated by Oliver Davis. New York: Routledge, 2004, 81–90.

———. *Phénomenologie de la Perception*. Paris: Gallimard, 2005. Translated into English by Donald A. Landes as *Phenomenology of Perception*. New York: Routledge, 2012.

———. "The Philosopher and His Shadow." In *Signs*. Translated by Richard C. McCleary. Evanston: Northwestern University Press, 1998, 159–81.

———. *The Structure of Behavior*. Translated by Alden Fisher. Boston: Beacon, 1967.

———. *The Visible and the Invisible*. Translated by Alphonso Lingis. Evanston: Northwestern University Press, 1997.

Morales, Michael, et al. "Gaze Following, Temperament, and Language Development in 6-Month-Olds: A Replication and Extension." *Infant Behavior and Development* 23 (2000): 231–36.

Morris, David. "The Enigma of Reversibility." *Continental Philosophy Review* 43 (2010): 141–65.

———. "The Open Figure of Experience and Mind." *Dialogue* 45 (2006): 315–26.

———. *The Sense of Space*. Albany: State University of New York Press, 2004.

Murphy, Ann V. "John Russon: Bearing Witness to Epiphany: Persons, Things, and the Nature of Erotic Life." *The Owl of Minerva* 41.1–2 (2009–10): 143–49.

Noë, Alva. *Action in Perception*. Cambridge, Massachusetts: MIT Press, 2004.

Ramachandran, V. S., and Sandra Blakeslee. *Phantoms in the Brain: Probing the Mysteries of the Human Mind*. New York: Morrow, 1998.

Reddy, Vasudevi. *How Infants Know Minds*. Cambridge, Massachusetts: Harvard University Press, 2010.

Rossmanith, N., et al. "Joint Structuring of Shared Spaces of Meaning and Action around Objects in Early Infancy: The Case of Book Sharing." *Frontiers in Psychology* 10 (2014): https://doi.org/10.3389/fpsyg.2014.01390.

Russon, John. *Bearing Witness to Epiphany*. Albany: State University of New York Press, 2009.

———. "Between Two Intimacies: The Formative Contexts of Adult Individuality." *Emotion, Space and Society* 13 (2014): 65–70.

———. "Embodiment and Responsibility: Merleau-Ponty and the Ontology of Nature." *Man and World* 27.3 (1994): 291–308.

———. "Freedom and Passivity: Attention, Work, and Language." In *Perception and Its Development in Merleau-Ponty's Phenomenology*. Edited by Kirsten Jacobson and John Russon. Toronto: University of Toronto Press, 2017, 25–39.

———. "Haunted by History: Merleau-Ponty, Hegel and the Phenomenology of Pain." *Journal of Contemporary Thought* 37 (2013): 81–94.

———. *Human Experience*. Albany: State University of New York Press, 2003.

———. "The Impossibilities of the I: Self, Memory, and Language in Merleau-Ponty and Derrida." In *Time, Memory, Institution: Merleau-Ponty's New Ontology of Self*. Edited by David Morris and Kym Maclaren. Athens, OH: University of Ohio Press, 2015, 91–105.

———. *Infinite Phenomenology*. Evanston: Northwestern University Press, 2016.

———. *Reading Hegel's Phenomenology*. Bloomington: Indiana University Press, 2004.

———. "The Right to Become an Individual." *Anekaant: A Journal of Polysemic Thought* 3 (2015): 17–22.

———. *Sites of Exposure: Art, Politics, and the Nature of Experience.* Bloomington: Indiana University Press, 2017.

———. "The Spatiality of Self-Consciousness." *Chiasmi International* 9 (2007): 209–20.

———. "The Virtue of Stoicism." *Dialogue* XLV (2006): 347–54.

———. "The Virtues of Agency: A Phenomenology of Confidence, Courage, and Creativity." In *Phenomenology and Virtue Ethics.* Edited by K. Hermberg and P. Gyllenhammer. New York: Bloomsbury, 2013, 165–79.

———. "Why Sexuality Matters." In *Desire, Love, and Identity: Philosophy of Sex and Love.* Edited by Gary Foster. Oxford: Oxford University Press, 2016, 38–48.

Salamon, Gayle. *Assuming a Body: Transgender and Rhetorics of Materiality.* New York: Columbia University Press, 2010.

Sartre, Jean-Paul. *Being and Nothingness.* Translated by Hazel Barnes. New York: Washington Square, 1992.

Scaife, M., and Bruner, J. S. "The Capacity for Joint Visual Attention in the Infant." *Nature* 253 (1975): 265–66.

Simms, Eva-Maria. "Intimacy and the Face of the Other: A Philosophical Study of Infant Institutionalization and Deprivation." *Emotion, Space and Society* 13 (2014): 80–86.

———. "Milk and Flesh: A Phenomenological Reflection on Infancy and Coexistence." *Journal of Phenomenological Psychology* 32.1 (2001): 22–40.

Smyth, Bryan. *Merleau-Ponty's Existential Phenomenology and the Realization of Philosophy.* London: Bloomsbury, 2014.

Sorce, James F., and Robert N. Emde. "Mother's Presence Is Not Enough: Effect of Emotional Availability on Infant Exploration." *Developmental Psychology* 17 (1981): 737–45.

Sorce, James F., et al. "Maternal Emotional Signaling: Its Effect on the Visual Cliff Behavior of 1-Year-Olds." *Development Psychology* 21 (1985): 195–200.

Stawarska, Beata. "Mutual Gaze and Social Cognition." *Phenomenology and the Cognitive Sciences* 5 (2006): 17–30.

Steinbock, Anthony. "Erotic Perception: Intersubjectivity, History and Shame." Published as "Perception érotique, histore et honte." *Alter: Revue de Phénoménologie* 20 (2012), 175–94.

———. *Home and Beyond: Generative Phenomenology after Husserl.* Evanston: Northwestern University Press, 1995.

Stern, Daniel. *The First Relationship.* Cambridge, Massachusetts: Harvard University Press, 1977.

———. *The Interpersonal World of the Infant.* New York: Basic Books, 1985.

Talero, Maria. "Merleau-Ponty and the Bodily Subject of Learning." *International Philosophical Quarterly* 46 (2006): 191–203.

Taylor, Charles. "Merleau-Ponty and the Epistemological Picture." In *The Cambridge Companion to Merleau-Ponty*. Edited by Taylor Carman and Mark B. Hansen. Cambridge: Cambridge University Press, 2005, 26–49.

Thompson, Evan. *Mind in Life*. Cambridge: Belknap, 2007.

Toombs, S. Kay. "The Lived Experience of Disability." *Human Studies* 18 (1995): 9–23.

Trevarthen, Colwyn. "Descriptive Analyses of Infant Communication Behavior." In *Studies in Mother-Infant Interaction: The Loch Lomond Symposium*. Edited by H. R. Schaffer. London: Academic (1975): 227–70.

Varela, Franciso J., Evan Thompson, and Eleanor Rosch. *The Embodied Mind*. Cambridge, Massachusetts: MIT Press, 1993.

Weiss, Gail. "The Normal, the Natural, the Normative: A Merleau-Pontian Legacy to Feminist Theory, Critical Race Theory, and Disability Studies." *Continental Philosophy Review* 48 (2015): 77–93.

Welsh, Talia. *The Child as Natural Phenomenologist*. Evanston: Northwestern University Press, 2013.

———. "The Developing Body: A Reading of Merleau-Ponty's Conception of Women in Sorbonne Lectures." In *Intertwinings: Interdisciplinary Encounters with Merleau-Ponty*. Edited by Gail Weiss. Albany: State University of New York Press, 2008, 45–59.

Welton, Donn. *The Other Husserl*. Bloomington: Indiana University Press, 2000.

Willett, Cynthia. *Interspecies Ethics*. New York: Columbia University Press, 2014.

———. *Maternal Ethics and Other Slave Moralities*. New York: Routledge, 1995.

Young, Iris Marion. "Throwing like a Girl." *Human Studies* 3.2 (1980): 137–56.

Zahavi, Dan. "Empathy and Mirroring: Husserl and Gallese." In *Life, Subjectivity and Art*. Edited by R. Breeur and U. Melle. New York: Springer, 2011, 217–54.

———. *Husserl and Transcendental Intersubjectivity: A Response to the Linguistic-Pragmatic Critique*. Translated by Elizabeth A. Behnke. Athens: Ohio University Press, 2001.

———. *Husserl's Phenomenology*. Stanford: Stanford University Press, 2003.

———. "Merleau-Ponty on Husserl: A Reappraisal." In *Merleau-Ponty's Reading of Husserl*. Edited by Ted Toadvine and Lester Embree. Dordrect: Kluwer, 2002, 3–29.

———. *Self-Awareness and Alterity: A Phenomenological Investigation*. Evanston: Northwestern University Press, 1999.

———. *Subjectivity and Selfhood*. Cambridge, Massachusetts: MIT Press, 2008.

Index

adulthood, 39, 42, 63, 65, 69, 71–72, 74, 96
agency, 40, 64, 67–69, 90
analogy, 46–47, 50
anticipation, 17–18, 21, 24–25
apprenticeship, 82
appresentation, 31, 33, 46, 48, 93
attraction, 73, 75–77, 85–87, 91
authentic erotic experience, 72, 83, 90–92
autonomy, 63, 85–87, 90
availability, 58, 60

Beauvoir, Simone de, 66, 72–73, 77, 81–85, 87, 90–92, 95
behavior, 11–15, 24–25, 28–30, 33, 36–38, 40–43, 45–52
being-in-the-world, 11–15, 17, 32, 39, 67, 94
being-with, 2, 39
betrayal, 72, 87–89
body: habitual, 15–17, 42; perceptive, 11–14, 17–18, 30–35, 46; in sexual experience, 72–77, 80–92; as way of being-in-the-world, 14–17
body schema, 12, 34, 43, 103n29; shared body schema, 34–38, 43, 103n29
bonds, 87–89, 95–96

Carr, Suzanne J., 58–59, 61
character, 19–22, 24–25, 96
childhood: intimacy, 73–74, 87; relation to neurotic behavior, 39–42; significance of, 64–69
collaboration, 37; between child and adult, 48–49, 50, 52, 62–64, 68; in recognition, 80; in sexual experience, 90–91
compulsion, 40, 42, 89
conflict, 22–24, 40, 42
consciousness: embodied, 10–17; intentionality of, 2, 5–11, 13; of other minds, 27–29; of other perceivers, 29; representational conception of, 5, 8
contact, 75, 81–86, 89–92
context: experiential, 3, 17, 19–23, 27, 39; interpersonal, 32, 39–45, 70, 91; perceptual, 7, 13
conversation, 19–20, 77
coordination, 55–56
creativity, 23–24, 30, 74; mutual, 89, 90–92, 95; primary creativity, 67

dance, 17, 21, 56–57
De Jaegher, Hanne, 62–63
dependence, 18, 64, 68, 85–87, 90–92
Descartes, René, 27

desire, 72–73, 75–78, 81–92
development: of agency, 64–69; of consciousness of other people, 28; of neurotic behavior, 39–42; of selfhood, 66–68, 73–74
Di Paolo, Ezequiel, 62–63
domination, 79–80, 84, 86, 88
dualism (mind-body), 14, 27, 40

eating, 41–42, 65
Emde, Robert N., 59–60
emotion, 53, 57–58, 60, 62–63, 67, 88
erotic experience. *See* sexuality
ethics, 4, 73, 92–96
expressivity, 81–85, 91–92, 111n26

facial expression, 38, 46–53, 55, 57, 61, 94
familiarity, 20, 41, 69, 74, 83, 94
family, 41–42, 65–66, 68–70, 73–74, 89
Feinman, Saul, 52
figure (and background), 6–7, 9, 23, 25, 27
flesh, 83–85
freedom, 41, 82, 89, 92, 94–96

Gallagher, Shaun, 49
Gelb, Adhemar, 76
Goldstein, Kurt, 76

habit, 20–25, 52, 89; embodied, 15–17, 81–82; interpersonal, 39–40, 69–70; neurotic, 39–41
hand, 83–85
harmony, 18–25, 38–40, 42, 71
Hegel, G. W. F., 73, 77–80, 84
Heidegger, Martin, 2, 11–13, 30, 32, 39, 47
honesty, 20–21, 87, 95
horizon, 7–10

Husserl, Edmund: experience of objects, 5–10; experience of other people, 29–34, 93; intentionality, 2, 5–11, 13, 72, 75; "pairing" relation, 3, 33–34, 43, 45–46, 52–53, 69

imperative, 10, 94–95
indeterminacy, 6–9, 76, 90
individuality, 20, 24, 35, 37, 43, 64–65, 68, 74, 95–96
initiation, 42, 64, 95
institution, 45, 64
intentionality: of consciousness, 2, 5–11, 13; motor, 30, 48; sexual, 72–73, 75–76, 81, 84, 86
interpretation, 24, 28, 67, 69
intersubjectivity: as dimension of perceptual experience, 4, 39–43; originary, 45, 64–70; primary vs. secondary, 53, 54; sexual, 72, 87, 92
intimacy, 64, 73–74, 87, 96

joint attention, 50–53

Laing, R. D., 66, 68
learning, 15–16, 36–37, 42, 69, 78
Levinas, Emmanuel, 94–95

master and slave relationship, 79–80, 86
melody, 18–21, 38–40, 96
Meltzoff, Andrew, 49
mental illness, 41
Merleau-Ponty, Maurice: "The Child's Relations with Others," 46; embodiment, 11–17, 34–38, 43, 74–77; lived space, 33; other people, 34–38, 43, 45–50, 52, 69; perceptual consciousness, 9–10; sexuality, 72–77, 80, 85–87

mind, 6, 10, 41, 46; other minds, 1, 27–29, 77; theory of, 28, 50; *See also* problem of other minds
mood, 47–48, 51–52, 57, 67
Moore, Keith, 49
movement, 10–11, 13–17, 28, 36, 49–52, 56–57, 82–85, 88
music, 17–21
mutual gaze, 50–52, 56, 62–63

narrative, 19
natural attitude, 5, 9
neonate imitation, 49–50, 52, 54
neurosis, 38, 40–42, 45, 68, 89
norm, 10, 72, 82, 88–92
normalcy, 40, 89–91, 105n43

objectivity, 10
orgasm, 83–84, 89
orientation, 30, 32–34, 102n16

pairing relation: adulthood, 72, 74, 96; *Cartesian Meditations*, 3, 29, 33, 34, 40, 43, 52; childhood, 45, 46, 49, 53, 54, 57, 58, 60, 61, 62, 72, 74, 96
participation: in collaborative experience, 37, 48–49, 52–53, 57, 63–64; in family life, 42, 68–69, 74; in sense making, 62–63
particularity, 3, 62, 68–69, 73–74
passivity, 82, 90
perception: embodied, 11–17, 30; existential significance of, 13–17; interpersonal significance of, 1, 38–43; of objects, 5–13; of other perceivers, 29–38, 48, 60–62, 93; representational conception of, 1, 6, 10, 30, 101n8
perspective: behavioral, 15–16, 24, 27; disparity between, 21–24; of others, 3, 31, 94; perceptual, 9–10; second-person, 54; third-person, 53
phantom limb, 14–15, 17, 42
phenomenology, 2–3, 25, 96
platform, 18, 24–25, 96
play periods, 54–57
politics, 4, 75
polytemporality, 2, 17, 19, 23, 38
possibility, 34–35, 37, 47, 50; as shared, 63, 65–66
problem of other minds, 1–2, 27, 31, 33–34, 54, 62, 103n24
profiles, 7–9
psychosis, 41, 68

reciprocity, 57, 80, 87–88, 91–92
recognition, 41, 66–68, 73, 77–87, 90, 92, 96
Reddy, Vasudevi, 28, 53–54
rejection, 84, 88
relationship: impersonal, 71; infant-caregiver, 3, 46–64; master-slave, 79–80, 86; parent-child, 21–24, 39–40, 65–66; *See also* sexuality; pairing relation; family
responsibility, 40, 84, 94–96
reversibility, 86
rhythm, 18–25, 38, 51–52, 71
Russon, John: childhood, 62, 64–69, 72–74; ethics, 95–96; mood, 47; neurosis, 38, 40–43, 45, 51, 89; polytemporality, 2–3, 17–23, 25, 38–39; sexuality, 72, 77, 87–91, 110n14

Sartre, Jean-Paul, 58
Schneider, Johann, 76–77, 86
self-consciousness, 12–13, 21, 37, 40, 67, 77–79
sexuality, 3–4, 70, 72–77, 80–92, 105n35

sharing: limits of, 35–36; meanings, 37–38; a world, 1, 36–37, 64, 68, 73; *See also* body schema: shared body schema
simulation theory, 28, 33
skin, 83–85
soccer, 36–37
social referencing, 52–54, 58
Sorce, James, 59–61, 65–66
spatiality, 32–33
Stawarska, Beata, 50
Stern, Daniel, 51, 54–58, 62–63
struggle, 79, 94
subjectivity, 1, 21, 27, 30, 37, 77–81
submission, 73, 79, 82–85

Talero, Maria, 15, 17
tempo, 51–52, 55, 63

temporality, 16–19; *See also* polytemporality
theory of mind theory (theory-theory), 28, 33
touch, 86, 86
transformation, 3, 5, 12, 16, 25, 38, 67, 70, 96
Trevarthen, Colwyn, 53–54
trust, 1, 3–4, 64, 72, 87, 92
typing, 15–16

virtue, 67
visual cliff, 61, 66
vulnerability, 73, 86–90, 92

walking, 11, 14–15
workshop, 30, 32, 57, 60

www.ingramcontent.com/pod-product-compliance
Lightning Source LLC
Chambersburg PA
CBHW052215240426
43670CB00037B/630